PRAISE FOR

The Gastronomy of Marriage

"*The Gastronomy of Marriage* is spirited, intimate, and great fun. Maisto writes with a vital contemporary frankness that belies a truly romantic spirit. The result is a wonderful marriage."

—ALEKSANDRA CRAPANZANO,
James Beard Award–winning writer

"Michelle Maisto's tender book traces the journey toward a momentous occasion—her wedding—with honesty, love, and vulnerability, all played out before, during, and after one mouthwatering meal after another."

—MATT MCALLESTER, author of *Bittersweet:
Lessons from My Mother's Kitchen*

"Lyrical, fresh, honest, and true, Maisto examines ˙˙˙ ˙˙˙ ˙ading up to her marriage with sincerity and inte˙˙ ˙˙˙ ˙˙ ˙˙˙ ˙˙ new light on the everyday dilemmas mo˙˙ ˙˙ ˙˙ ˙˙˙ ˙˙ ˙˙ ˙ek to nourish themselves and the˙ ˙˙˙ ˙˙˙ ˙˙ ˙˙˙ ˙˙˙ ˙˙ from Maisto's Italian Ame˙˙ ˙˙ ˙˙ ˙˙ ˙˙ ˙˙ ˙˙ ˙be's Chinese American heritage, ˙ ˙˙ ˙˙ ˙˙ ˙˙˙ ˙˙viting, and the love story—as American ˙ ˙˙ ˙˙ ˙˙˙erly captivates. A must-read for anyone who has n˙˙ ˙˙ ˙˙e complicated waters of coupling, from beginning to end."

—KAMY WICOFF, author of *I Do But I Don't:
Why the Way We Marry Matters*

RANDOM HOUSE

TRADE

PAPERBACKS

New York

The
GASTRONOMY
of MARRIAGE

A MEMOIR
of
FOOD AND
LOVE

MICHELLE
MAISTO

A Random House Trade Paperback Original

Copyright © 2009 by Michelle Maisto

Published in the United States by
Random House Trade Paperbacks,
an imprint of The Random House Publishing Group,
a division of Random House, Inc., New York.

RANDOM HOUSE TRADE PAPERBACKS and colophon
are trademarks of Random House, Inc.

Maisto, Michelle.
The gastronomy of marriage: a memoir of
food and love / Michelle Maisto.
p. cm.
ISBN 978-0-8129-7919-0
1. Food habits—United States. 2. Chinese Americans—Food.
3. Italian Americans—Food. 4. Interethnic marriage—United States.
5. Maisto, Michelle. I. Title.
GT2853.U5M35 2009
394.1'2—dc22   2009005684

Printed in the United States of America

www.atrandom.com

2 4 6 8 9 7 5 3 1

Book design by Barbara M. Bachman

To Rich,
for his love, support,
and friendship.
And to my mother,
for everything.

It seems to me that our three basic needs,
for food and security and love, are so mixed and
mingled and entwined that we cannot straightly think
of one without the others. So it happens that when
I write of hunger, I am really writing about love and the
hunger for it, and warmth and the love of it and the
hunger for it . . . and then the warmth and richness and
fine reality of hunger satisfied . . . and it is all one.

— M. F. K. FISHER, *The Art of Eating*

Contents

...

Introduction · *xi*

CHAPTER 1
January · *3*

CHAPTER 2
Dinner Takes All · *13*

CHAPTER 3
Chineseification · *38*

CHAPTER 4
February · *53*

CHAPTER 5
In the Neighborhood · *70*

CHAPTER 6
The Beef · *89*

CHAPTER 7
Together, Apart · *100*

CHAPTER 8
March · *123*

CHAPTER 9

Apples and Oranges · *132*

CHAPTER 10

A Dinner Party Is Borne · *141*

CHAPTER 11

Holiday · *164*

CHAPTER 12

April · *189*

CHAPTER 13

Sickness and Health · *199*

CHAPTER 14

Risotto, Frittata, Fried Rice · *211*

CHAPTER 15

May · *221*

Acknowledgments · *235*

Introduction

...

I WAS TOLD TO MARRY A MAN FOR HIS HEART (OR MORE exactly, his soul), but in the end it was a stomach I fell for. On our first date, Rich ordered a chocolate soufflé at the beginning of the meal, noting an asterisk on the menu warning diners of the wait involved. At the time, I imagined he did it partly to impress me, which it did, though today I know well that he's simply the type of man who knows better than to turn down a hot-from-the-oven soufflé when one is offered to him.

That the latter was a necessary quality in any person I might consider marrying was something I likely knew somewhere inside me but couldn't have put into words that day. I was twenty-two and having an early dinner in a breezy Los Angeles restaurant on Sunset and Vine, with a co-worker I'd kissed two nights before, tipsy on tequila after a postwork Memorial Day party. Even so, I felt the importance of this new information—that he was a good eater, and an eater I could respect—and, despite having spent the previous five months working together and hanging out very platonically, hiking trails in Malibu and the Valley, it struck me as the most significant definer of his character that I'd so far been privy to, and I felt more connected to him for it.

Today I have a clearer sense of what attracts me, and sitting with a poor eater, the articulated words *impotent* and *emasculated* come to me, cruel as they are. Even as a young girl, I sometimes felt a jolt of meanness toward fussy eaters. Being a good eater was a point of pride in my family, and there were summer nights when I sat alongside my father eating more steamer clams than I cared for—using the ugly black siphons that poked from their shells to dip them first in hot water, to rinse them, and then in a ramekin of melted butter—simply to bask longer in his approval. My sisters, both decent eaters, drew the line at the steamers' texture and scrunched their faces in disgust; but I was my father's daughter, and we ate on.

We have always been a warm, boisterous, physical family—hugging and kissing and linking arms and sitting close—but we can also be a quietly judgmental lot, who frown at weakness and prize strength above all else. And there are no more egregious revealers of a weak nature than being fussy at the table, straying from one's faith, and staying with a man you know isn't right for you. By which I mean dating; in marriage, it was understood, one was sealed to one's mistakes.

I've heard it said that "love chooses you," but I was raised to believe it's a choice each of us makes—*the* most important choice each of us makes—and that the consequence of not doing so properly can be a life more akin to a long, unhappy death. George Washington, of all people, once put it nicely when he wrote to a friend: "I have always considered marriage as the most interesting event of one's life, the foundation of happiness or misery." As a girl I watched my aunts and neighbors with their husbands, and my older cousins marry, and I saw how the person you chose, like a dye dropped into water, came to affect everything.

My eye was trained to this by my mother, who by her own admission had chosen poorly. She and my father dated for a year, and after enough people asked when they were going to get married, in the car after a date one night my father said, "So I guess we should get married." And my mother agreed. She mostly blamed her decision on not having anyone to talk it over with. She still tells me, incredulous, "It wasn't until we were at the church and Grandma was *pulling the veil down over my face* that she said to me, 'Are you sure about this?' " By the time they reached their honeymoon, my mother was certain of her mistake.

Determined to protect her three daughters from similar fates, she filled the talk in our household of women (which certainly it was even before my father left, during our teenage years) with tales and dissections of relationships and marriage. It was an agenda further fueled by my older sister, Bridget, who was particularly pretty and so attracted the attention of men quite early (far earlier than my younger sister, Maria, or I would, which I think actually suited us both). At the center of all the talk was usually a woman who *just didn't understand* what she was getting into; or who was so in love she *simply couldn't see* a situation for what it was. I understood early that men possessed the ability to separate a woman from her senses, and that in order to choose correctly I would have to keep my mind and eyes clear so as not to become a victim of the very thing I sought to commit to.

I stepped carefully through a modest dating career, and then one January afternoon Rich walked into the office of my first magazine job, to interview for the position just above mine. I was the editorial assistant, with a big desk up front for secretarial chores, and I handed him the paperwork, validated his parking ticket, and told him to sit and wait. Back then, the type of man who turned my head was thick and athletic, a bulk of a man in whose enormous hands I felt feminine and light. This person who chose the chair closest to my desk, however, extending and crossing his legs at the ankles, so that twice I had to step over them, was just a head taller than me, broad-shouldered but thin, confident but eager; I imagined myself out of his league. And still, with a severity I couldn't explain even to myself, catching the strangeness of my actions, I made a point of ignoring him: disliking how casually he'd dressed; aware he wasn't fidgeting like the others; disregarding the neat curve of his black hair around his small, perfect ears.

The first time I went to his apartment, I noticed a DVD of *A Room with a View* on his television, which is a book I love and a movie that few people have ever agreed to watch with me. I've been a fervent reader since I was in single-digit birthdays, disappearing deep inside a book only to look up hours later in a nearly dark room, queasy and discombobulated with the feeling of being so abruptly returned to my life. I can still see my mother turning at the sink with a white dish towel in her hands, a look of surprise on her face as I walked, squinting, into the bright kitchen, my cheeks hot with indignant tears over the unfair treatment of poor Ramona Quimby, age eight. Years later, it was Lucy Honeychurch I particularly related to, and with her I fell in love with George Emerson. A decade after first seeing the movie, I still pined for a man who could kiss me with the urgency that

George kissed Lucy in the field of violets; a man who could love me with such urgency.

"Is that yours?" I asked him.

"Yeah, I love that movie," he said. "Have you seen it?"

Rich has a theory that the universe (or as I think of it, God) sets out little signposts for us along the way, to confirm that we're on the right path. Had I known this theory then, the moment definitely would have qualified.

We dated for two years before, frustrated with my career, I decided to apply to graduate schools. We were happy and I loved him and I was *in* love with him, but I was still too young, I imagined, to be thinking about marriage, so I applied to the schools I wanted to go to, regardless of where they were, because while I didn't want to leave him, I was even more adamant about not being the type of woman who made important decisions based on a man. "The intellect is always fooled by the heart," La Rochefoucauld knew as early as the seventeenth century. But I told myself I was keeping my head clear.

During the months that we waited for the universities' replies, I thought about how, had the situation been reversed—had he applied for something that meant leaving me—I would have been incredibly hurt. And I knew, too, that had he applied to something far away and asked me to go with him I likely would have refused, entirely out of pride. I would have left someone I loved before I gave anyone the ammunition to say, *And then she just gave up everything and followed him.* I wouldn't have done it, and I didn't ask him to.

Still, when Columbia accepted me I whispered to Rich during a late-night call, "Did they just put an expiration date on us?" But he surprised me. "I'll move too," he said. "I'll get an apartment near yours and work freelance. I want to be with you." By then he was the editor in chief of the magazine where we'd met and had turned it into one of the company's most profitable. His contract kept him there another ten months after I moved, but the week it was up he packed his things and left Los Angeles for New York. Or rather, he left Los Angeles for me.

Four years later I turned in a thesis, and the week of my May graduation Rich pulled a ring from the front pocket of his jeans and made a nervous but earnest speech I hope I always remember. It was six years to the day from our first kiss. We found an apartment, signed a lease for July 1, and finally moved in together.

Moving in together is a thing I suppose we might have done sooner, but I was raised in fire-and-brimstone churches and still possess enough God fear to want to keep certain carts behind certain horses. As a sixth or seventh grader back in evangelical churches, I used to hope the apocalypse wouldn't really happen in the year 2000, as my mother said it likely would, so that I'd still have a chance at some God-sanctioned married sex. My understanding of sex at the time was, at best, absolutely vague, but it still struck me as incredibly unfair that I might rise up into heaven before adulthood and be made to miss out on this thing that everyone else seemed to enjoy so enormously. In the end, my carts and horses weren't always arranged exactly as my mother and God might have liked (I can barely remember a time when they weren't a team), and even now, our living together before the wedding, engaged or not, raises more eyebrows than I care to consider.

The apartment we moved into is on the western edge of Brooklyn, in an ugly, industrial neighborhood that's not without its charms. As manufacturing headed overseas, artists moved into the emptied factories lining these streets, and the young and entrepreneurial eventually followed, opening cocktail bars with silver absinthe drippers and mustachioed bartenders, pork-only barbecue restaurants, and the types of intricately detailed boutiques that girls dream up in their bedrooms. Our building was once a knitting factory run by our landlord's father, and our ground-floor apartment—a vaguely S-shaped open loft with high ceilings and windows only in the bedroom area—is where I suspect the loading dock once stood. Across the street is a still-functioning factory for wooden water towers (the odd, silo-like structures that sit so incongruously atop apartment buildings), and from our bed we can see its tall chute and hear and smell the mulched wood it sends sliding down. To the left, though—compensation—the street widens and the view is a welcome swath of sky, a churning stretch of the East River, and the startling profile of Manhattan's East Side: the Union Square clock tower, the changing colored lights of the Empire State Building that click off at midnight sharp, and the racing lines of the FDR Drive, with its marching ants by day and double strands of pearls each night.

The soufflé is all I remember about the dinner portion of that first date, both his ordering it and how ethereal its warm top later was in my mouth. Though I can still feel the shy nervousness with which I entered the restaurant, and see the late-evening sun that glinted off my windshield when Rich walked me to my car (we had driven separately, straight from work). And I can too well still conjure the horrible, wonderful whir that took over my chest, a mixture of anxiousness and longing and a great need to secure something elemental and wholly necessary that ran inside me like a small motor on high, undoing me for weeks until I felt sure that he was mine and I was his and whatever it was we had started with that kiss would last for some good amount of time.

Just how much time, I was fuzzy on, but I pictured something solid and reflective of the growing love that I felt—maybe an entire year, or even two. But never did I imagine that the skinny, confident twenty-six-year-old ordering that soufflé for us—the only one of the handful of young guys at our office who had visited my desk and noticed my tattered copy of *One Hundred Years of Solitude* and had already read it himself—was the man I was going to marry. Or that, smiling at me across the starched white tablecloth, with the kitchen door and a sloping potted palm over his left shoulder, was the person I'd hope to be sharing my meals with always.

THE
GASTRONOMY OF
MARRIAGE

THE FIRST SATURDAY OF 2005 (THE YEAR OF THE WOODEN Rooster on the Chinese calendar, which is predicting a holdover of grudges) is clear and cold, with a bright, misleading sun that makes each of us anxious to get outside. Union Square is a quick three stops on the L train, so we head to the farmers' market, where, when we manage to stay in full sun, the winter air seems not so bad.

In the northwest corner, where Christmas trees were propped two weeks ago, plain pine wreaths are still being peddled. "Good luck to them," Rich says quietly, echoing my thoughts. An ardent celebrator, even I have reached my tolerance for sweeping up pine needles. Rich dragged our little tree to the park a week ago, where the city was mulching them for free, and I stayed behind to sweep and vacuum, happy to reclaim those few feet of space and enjoying the pine scent coming from the warm machine.

Today there are two farms selling apples, a woman with honey, an upstate winery pouring Riesling and ice wine, plus stands with organic beef, goat cheeses and milks, free-range eggs, and green sodlike squares of wheatgrass. A stand with glass breadboxes filled with baked goods is swarmed, but a woman selling pickles sits alone behind her table with a brave face. I feel a pang of embarrassment for her, a silly response. I can't even bear to throw yard sales, so squeamish is my aversion to selling things—an elitist-sounding affliction, perhaps, but one likely traceable to feeling pressured to hand out religious tracts at my hometown county fair when I was twelve or thirteen, an age at which being called on in class was enough to turn me scarlet.

The crowd is slow-moving, filled with bicycles, dogs in more fashionable coats than I own, and heavy-duty baby strollers—perfect for transporting pounds of root vegetables and tall funnels of blue-green eucalyptus, if the baby doesn't mind. What could we do with tight, pretty Brussels sprouts, still on their stalks? It's a vegetable I always want to like, though I still see the single sprout that my fourth-grade teacher hung in a sandwich bag from the strip of cork above the blackboard—a gift from a student, after he'd made his disdain for them known. It hung there until we left for the summer, turning every color and finally growing a soft fur. Rich likes the look of these long piled stalks as well, but it's a relief when he suggests they might just stink up the kitchen.

A farm from upstate is selling apples, carrots, celeriac, winter squashes, apple-cider doughnuts, and steaming cups of apple cider from immense, sticky pots. (I don't envy whoever gets to scrub these tonight.) A long ladle goes in and we each get a cup. For a dollar more we buy a clear sandwich bag of three golden doughnuts—cake style and rolled in cinnamon and sugar—and take them into the park beside the market to share on a bench. This takes us out of the sun, but we sit close and warm our hands around our cups. A perfect Saturday.

And still the thought comes to me: Can we stay this happy? It's a question that I press down as quickly as it pops up. As a young girl, I would wake from naps and find my mother sitting on the carpeted steps where the sun hit during the late afternoon and nuzzle into her, still shaking off sleep. "Close your eyes," she'd say, her face lifted to the sun, "and you can be anywhere. Where do you want to be?" Always she chose somewhere warm and far away. But Catholics didn't divorce, and so she stayed and stayed.

These days I find I've become our relationship's barometer, its dedicated lighthouse keeper, my finger licked and lifted to every shift of mood, change of tone. The lessons my mother drilled into her daughters aren't easy to shake. Is it possible that I'm blind and don't know it? Could I really say "I do" and only then have the blinders fall away, revealing some terrible fate I've sealed myself to? A part of me continually circles back to these questions, as no-nonsense an inspection as the one I perform each morning—keys? wallet? phone?—before heading out the door, assured that the day is on track.

Rich finishes his doughnut, switches his cider to his right hand, and puts his left arm around me, to warm and hug me closer. *We're happy,* I tell myself. *Things are good.*

We take a final turn around the market and pick up apples, an acorn squash, and a damp bundle of carrots with their feathery greens still attached. "How about *pasta e fagioli* for dinner?" I suggest, and amazingly Rich agrees. Sun or not, an hour in the cold has made us both hungry for the same type of meal. At my mother's table, *pasta e fagioli,* like beef stew and minestrone, would call for buttered popovers, their hollow innards perfect for scooping up stew or wiping the dregs from a bowl. They're easy to make, but we agree to keep things simpler still—the dirty dishes to a minimum—so while I pay for the carrots Rich maneuvers back through the crowd for a baguette from the bread stand.

Our meals are rarely transitioned into as easily as soup on a winter day. I've begun wondering if this is because when a person eats alone, two eggs go a long way toward a respectable dinner. They're filling, they don't cost much, they come individually portioned, they're actually protein (versus the cheap carbohydrates that fill most cupboards), and they aren't much trouble to make or clean up afterward. Before we moved in together, I would happily scramble a few eggs, or make an omelet with a bit of cheese in the fold, and eat it alongside a handful of dressed salad greens, a toasted slice of good bread, and a glass of wine if there was an open bottle in the house. Or, if the greens involved frisée, I might toss them with only vinegar, salt, and pepper, poach the eggs or fry them gently, and then put them over the greens, letting their pierced yolks dribble down, acting as the dressing's silky fat. The cheese could then go over the bread, be shown the inside of the broiler, and be eaten as a bubbly, open-faced cheese sandwich. *Bliss!* That all this changes once there's a second person at the table somehow caught me by surprise.

I used to walk from the subway back to 9J, my shared graduate-student apartment, thinking, *What can I eat . . . ? What can I eat . . . ?* Then I'd remember the eggs, the ciabatta roll left over from breakfast, that there were loose greens in the crisper, and that would be that. Forty seconds of preoccupied thought, and ten of those were imagining the rapturous moment of dipping the spongy ciabatta innards into a dripping yolk. But in the context of our new grown-up home, a dinner of eggs suddenly seems less fitting. Though even if I were up for it—the walk, the thought, the plan—all can be moot if he had eggs for breakfast; or if he's particularly hungry and thinks this doesn't sound filling; or even if he's simply not in the mood. Which, honestly, is a thing I can't argue much with. Even Elizabeth David, the author of *An Omelette and a Glass of Wine,* and a proponent of such a meal if ever there was one, believed that much of the pleasure of food and wine comes from "having what you want *when* you want it, and in the particular combination you fancy."

People had warned me, during those years of separate apartments: *You learn new things about a person when you live together.* Friends, acquaintances at parties, strangers in line at the pharmacy—with little to no provocation they had flashed this hard-won nugget at me like a badge. But at the table, Rich and I have long understood each other. We're both game to drive all morning for a lunch of cracked crabs on newspaper, look forward to persimmon season as eagerly as to any holiday, and think trolling the aisles of foreign grocery stores is a normal part of any vacation. For my birthday our first year together, he planned the evening so that we had fresh seafood appetizers at a motorcycle bar in Malibu, and then completed the meal at a more formal restaurant down the coast. (The other part of the gift was a first-edition Márquez novel; surely cartoon hearts beat in my eyes that night.)

And still, by August I did begin to discover things. Small things. That he likes his ketchup in the pantry, instead of in the refrigerator, where I like it. That he likes cereal but not for breakfast. He likes soy milk but not in his cereal. And he likes to hurry even apples to the crisper, instead of arranging them in a pretty bowl on the counter, because he's sure they'll spoil instantly and attract fruit flies. The peanut butter shuttled between the baking cabinet and the refrigerator door for two weeks before the conversation was had that I prefer it chunky and cold but he likes it warm and creamy. What is the marriage protocol for such things? Were we supposed to buy both kinds, or was one of us supposed to shrug off our preference . . . for as long as we both shall live? The question trickled down to even the little trash can in the bathroom, which I like to eventually empty into a larger trash bag but he likes to line with a bag, most often a plastic grocery bag, that covers over the little can entirely and looks terrible. If I gave in now, could there be any reversing this later? Was I giving in forever?

People had also insisted to me that when couples got married things changed from the way they were when they were dating. My mother frequently remarked that I should make sure I really liked Rich as a person, because all the "tingly romantic feelings" I felt now would surely someday disappear. And still others urged me forward. At the wedding of my childhood best friend (who went from single to committed, engaged, and then married through the third and fourth years of my relationship), her mother squeezed my arm and whispered, "Marriage is a good thing, just go for it!" But not one of them pointed out that there is actually no reason to expect that two people who grew up in different households, with naturally different traditions and approaches to eating and meals, and who have ethnically different versions of comfort foods, varying ideologies about what is acceptable to consume, and bodies with vastly different metabolisms and digestive traits, should easily be able to sit to the same meal each night. And yet this is what we now negotiate.

Rich eats meat, but I don't. My iron gut could digest a muffler, but his rebukes him for tomato sauce, carbonation, eating quickly. He prefers the light, clean flavors that his mother learned as a girl, watching the family chef in China, while I tend toward the hearty dishes of my father's childhood in Southern Italy. And although Rich hasn't seen the inside of a locker room since junior high, the carbohydrates in a meal of straight-up pasta bounce off him, while the moment I stop jogging they take up long-term accommodations on my hips and thighs. These details had always existed, eating in restaurants and hosting each other in our separate apartments, but six months into living together they've taken on new gravity. Since the moving van touched the curb, I'd been waiting for the long-promised surprise to emerge, and finally each of us could see what it was: We love to eat, and to eat together, but dinner every night, in a home of our creation, was turning out to be something else.

To be fair, my mother did warn me, repeatedly, that marriage is all about compromise. I just never fathomed that these compromises—mature acts of finding a middle ground that as a girl I imagined myself and my perfect husband acting out with selfless patience—would happen with such frequency. And never did I imagine that the bulk of them would be over dinner.

The carrots could do with just a good scrubbing, but I like the texture of them peeled, which takes less time anyway.

The trick is to peel toward oneself, though I can't help but like that it's so many people's instinct to peel away from themselves instead; it seems very survivalist, or Darwinian, that we should more naturally draw the knife away. I quarter two of the carrots lengthwise, chop them into triangles, and sauté them in olive oil with a chopped onion and two diced celery ribs. After a few minutes, I add four bulbs of minced garlic, and before it can brown I pour in vegetable stock, canned cannellini beans, the empty can's worth of water, a squeeze of tomato paste from a tube, and a bay leaf. "Watch out for the bay leaves!" rings in my ears each time I pull one from the jar, trying to keep its brittle tip intact. My mother, endlessly terrified that one of us would choke on these dusty-looking leaves, attached an ominousness to them that they've yet to be relieved of.

Once the stock is simmering and the vegetables are soft, I pull out the bay leaf, purée half the soup in the blender to make the whole thing heartier, and add a cup of cooked shell macaroni, more ground pepper, and a handful of roughly grated Pecorino. Old Italian ladies fastidiously save the heels of their hard cheeses for just such occasions, but they don't have Rich scrubbing the bottoms of their pots after dinner and insisting, "Why can't we just sprinkle the Parmesan over our bowls at the end? It tastes *exactly* the same!"

I dress a salad of baby spinach with dried prunes and almonds, and Rich toasts slices of the baguette in the broiler—which we've learned to make do with, since neither of us owns a toaster—and then drizzles them with olive oil and thick kosher salt. Normally, I can't shake the feeling that I'm still sixteen and faking my way through the adult world, but ladling up this very-not-chic favorite of grandmothers, I can't help but feel grown-up. Rich opens a Chianti and finally we sit, say grace (or rather I do, always this falls to me) and touch glasses.

"*Buon appetito*," I say.

"To the chef," he answers. And we dig in.

POPOVERS

> *2 eggs*
> *1 cup milk*
> *1 tablespoon butter, melted*
> *½ teaspoon salt*
> *1 cup all-purpose flour*

PREHEAT THE OVEN TO 450 DEGREES. Sift the flour if you have the time. Otherwise, simply put everything in the blender, the flour last, and pulse until *just* combined. Then put the blender container in the refrigerator for 10 minutes and a muffin tin in the hot oven for 5. Take out the muffin tin and spray it with nonstick spray or brush it with butter (if you leave the tin in longer than 5 minutes, the butter or spray will burn, which is a lousy way to start out), and then fill each cup halfway with batter. Bake for 15 minutes, then lower the oven to 375 and bake for 15 minutes more. Don't take the popovers out of the oven until they're lightly browned and forming the slightest crust—or, even more subtly, a *structural integrity*—or they'll deflate. Once you do take them out, the gentle insertion of a sharp toothpick into each top is said to further prevent them from falling. Serve warm with butter. Makes five or six, which serves two. If you're already going to the trouble, though, you may as well double the recipe and look forward to breakfast.

...

THE PASTA WATER IS ALREADY BOILING WHEN RICH announces he needs cream. A decade ago he lived in Paris with a culinary-student roommate, and now he has a knack with sauces and reductions, things I'm clueless about; but clam sauce is Italian and I have eaten my share. "What does cream have to do with clam sauce?" I ask again, but I'm shooed from the stove. After some deliberation, he concedes to make do with half-and-half, and he flips together the clams, the linguini, and the half-and-half in the air with quick, circular jerks on the pan.

It's his night to cook, but he tends to overlook a vegetable component—the component I care about most—and so, relegated to the triangle of countertop beside the sink, I make a spinach salad with blue cheese and Roma apples I bought from the grocer up the block, who was particularly forlorn about the truckload of them someone had sold her, all bad at the bottom. At forty-nine cents a pound, she encouraged me to buy more, but their skins didn't look taut and I told her I was afraid they were going to be mealy.

"What is 'mealy'?" she asked. She has a thick Israeli accent that to my ears sounds like Bullwinkle's Natasha.

"You know," I said, "when it's not crisp, when it's . . ." I made a chewing face and rubbed together the fingers of one hand in a way that seemed to convey gritty.

"Ahh . . ." she said, understanding and nodding her head a few times with the emphasis on the backward motion, which I liked. Where a forward nod might be suppliant, the backward nod felt appraising, which struck me as cute—an unlikely adjective for this woman who keeps her creased, unhappy face down on her crossed arms between customers.

"If they're not mealy, I'll come back for more," I told her, and she gave me one pronounced forward nod to indicate this was fair.

The apples are blooming patches of rust before I can peel and slice through a whole one, so I surrender and toss them through the vinaigrette on the bottom of the salad bowl and pile the spinach and blue cheese gently on top, to toss through when we're ready to eat them. Rich chops through a few wands of flat parsley and joins Mick Jagger on the chorus, insisting he's not waiting on a lady. Then he flips everything into the air again, the leaves disappearing inside the folds of linguini, and announces that dinner is ready.

The clams were a last-minute decision, coming after Rich squatted for a long stare into the pantry cabinet beside the stove, tapping his front tooth with his forefinger the way he does when forming the last bit of a plan. Which is my new favorite sight: the man I love taking the reins of dinner. It makes me feel buoyed, empowered; fit for a propaganda poster in which I'm striding with renewed confidence toward the great unknown of marriage. Rich wishes aloud for a second time that he'd had fresh ones to work with, but canned clams, half-and-half and all, the results are such that in no time our plates are empty again. Even the spinach and blue cheese go quickly, though neither of us finishes the apples.

Normally we linger at the table, but tonight we're both eager to get to the movie he rented, the original *Italian Job,* so together we clean up quickly, top off our glasses with the last of the sauvignon blanc that went into the clams, and settle into the couch, arranging ourselves under a big white blanket so it covers us from our chins to our feet, propped side by side on the coffee table. "In New York you can hear any kind of live music, any night of the week. Eat any kind of cuisine. See ballet, opera, sing karaoke," I tell the people who question why, with school finished, I'd want to stay in this expensive, cramped city. "It's all going on, all the time, with people from all over the world!" Though in truth, more nights than not this is exactly where I can be found. Which is just fine with me.

Halfway through we pause the movie, and I get up to slice dessert, a spongy brown apple cake that I baked before dinner, its caramelized-sugar scent quickly giving way to the more pungent garlic and clams. I leave off the overhead light, having always liked the feeling of a kitchen that's been put to bed for the night: the sink empty and scrubbed, the dinner dishes standing quietly in the drying rack, the countertop a shiny runway wiped clean of crumbs and junk mail and water glasses, and only the bulb over the stove, or maybe a dim sink light, making it easy to maneuver for a final glass of water. Even by the glow of the television it's clear this cooperative old recipe was a much better fit for the Depressed Grocer's apples.

Plating the slices, I feel the satisfaction of having something special efficiently waiting, literally on the back burner—which is very "my mother" of me. As a girl, I worried whether I'd someday be able to do all she did, as well as she did it. Pin a hem, sew a costume, cut hair, have a snack and a Band-Aid and a tissue at the ready. Would I be able to make the special butterfly cookies for bake sales, dipping the butterfly-shaped frame on its long wand into batter and then sizzling oil, and then loosening the suddenly crisp confection from the frame, ever so gently? A neighbor woman had once commented—offering a compliment along with a barb, which my mother had felt— on how my mother was always put together so nicely, and first thing in the morning, and that our house was always clean and everything perfect. I worried, too, whether I would know how to be perfect.

"Oh, excellent cake!" Rich says, taking his eyes off the movie to smile at me. After years of setting myself up for such compliments, I've begun to realize what a baldly self-congratulating thing it is to plate up an item that's sure to please; how baking in particular is almost entirely about creating an unnecessary but welcome treat with which to make other people sit up happily and thank you. How much of my pleasure in the kitchen is tied to these congratulatory pats? The photos of me tipping rabbit-shaped cakes toward the camera at Easter, or stuffed chocolate logs at Christmas, extend back to elementary school.

Rich puts his empty plate and fork on the side table with a little clatter and settles back into the couch and the blanket and me until we're cozily situated. He is a big fan of cozy. "Oh, that's cozy," he'll say happily, once we've turned off the light, shifted around, and settled into bed for the night. If I sit up for a sip of water and undo things, "That's not cozy," comes the verdict. A slight adjustment. "Oh, cozy . . ." he'll say, and I can feel him smiling delightedly in the darkness.

The tiny cars zip through Turin, the bus lurches around mountain passes, and under the blanket we're holding hands. Encouraged by the smooth-sailing successes of canned clams and apple cake, I catch myself smugly wondering if maybe this will be a marriage that defies the odds, and possibly the wrath of God, and actually works out.

. . .

YASMINE, MY PAKISTANI graduate-school roommate, married her Swedish boyfriend, Patrik, while we were still living in 9J. Patrik was offered a teaching position in Bologna that year, though, so Yasmine and I kept on living together, with Patrik joining us during holidays and long breaks. It was an arrangement I couldn't have minded any less. They're sweet and smart and interesting, and I adore them both. Plus, it was fun to be part of a happy marriage, while spared the more stressful bits, like the difficulty of two economists finding work in the same city.

Tonight, Patrik calls from D.C., where they're both working for the year, to say he might be up for the day soon, and we discuss the possibility of having a drink before he catches his train home. Before we hang up, I pause and then ask him, "What did you two have for dinner last night?" For Patrik, home foods are clean, fresh flavors: buttermilk, berries, brisk pickled herring with cold potatoes and dill; whereas the foods Yasmine most happily sits to are spicy, slow-cooked amalgams of blooming, layered flavors. During our four years together in 9J, the four of us made and sat to countless meals, played increasingly competitive rounds of Scrabble, danced to overly loud Bollywood mixes until the doorman came knocking, and plotted how we might continue to live commune style indefinitely, eventually homeschooling our kids, with each of us responsible for a subject. If they've figured out how to deal with the nightly issue of dinner—working around their differing tastes, and sans a housewife to see to the cooking—there are no coattails I'm more comfortable grabbing hold of.

"Um, last night we ordered in," he says. "We both worked late."

"Well, what about the night before?"

He laughs sheepishly. "We ordered in."

Rich and I order in or eat out a few nights a week as well, but sitting to a proper dinner most nights—television off, a set table, the expectation of conversation—has been an unspoken part of the grown-up lives we imagined for ourselves. Through the summer months first settling into the apartment, we happily took turns with the housework and the cooking, each of us going out of our way to please the other. (*Look how modern we are! How good we are at this!*) But gradually, thinking about and shopping for and preparing dinner has become tiring, especially after a full day of work. And it's become tiring, too, to be so agreeable and accommodating, especially at home, where a person wants to relish in being her truest, most comfortable self. Which is part of why I broke down earlier and brought home broccoli rabe from the market.

There are days I crave bitter greens like a thirst. They feel to me to be the most intense kind of sustenance, like the medicinal tonics in old cartoons, shooting steam from the ears but sprouting muscles by the armload. I like them hot from the skillet, heavy on garlic, and with the type of crusty bread that would scrape the mouth were it not for the pan juices to mop up. My mother can't eat broccoli rabe without saying how she hated it as a girl, but her mother bought it literally by the bushel, to meet the demands of their sprawling dinner table, and now there's nothing she likes more than a breakfast of cold broccoli rabe with the end of a loaf of Italian bread that's been left on the counter overnight. Her father, too, liked the type of crunch that makes one worry for one's teeth.

I didn't develop a taste for these greens until my early twenties, and looking over the produce one day at the old Westside Market on West 110th Street, below Columbia—the type of market that made me giddy to my bones to finally be a New Yorker—I called my mother. "What was that bitter thing we used to eat?" I asked.

"Brocoletti di rape," she said. "Or sometimes the stores call it broccoli rabe, or rapini."

I brought some back to 9J, sautéed it in garlic, olive oil, red-pepper flakes, and a squeeze of lemon, as she'd instructed me to, tossed it with grated Parmesan and orecchiette (the macaroni called little ears, though to me they always look more like sombreros), and served it to Yasmine, Patrik, and Rich, all of whom immediately recoiled at the bitterness.

"Whoa!" Rich had gasped, making a face like he'd been pepper-sprayed. "Oh, my . . ." Yasmine said softly. I think Patrik only smiled at me sympathetically. But I loved it.

"Maybe you just need more cheese," I told them, tearing another slice of bread from the loaf on the table. But unless I was eating alone, that was the end of broccoli rabe in that apartment.

Tonight, I paired it instead with thick spaghetti, and blanched it in the boiling pasta water to reduce the bitterness. But when Rich stood to carry our plates to the sink afterward, he still said nicely, "Maybe we can eat that a little less often. . . ."

"Really? I blanched it. You still didn't like it?"

"It was *okay*," he said diplomatically.

I picked the last lettuce leaves from the salad bowl, and he scraped spaghetti strands into the trash; our hard-and-fast rule is that whoever does the cooking, the other person does the cleaning up.

"You know, in *The Man Who Ate Everything*, Jeffrey Steingarten says that most food aversions can be overcome by eating a thing just eight to ten times," I offered. Steingarten, the food critic for *Vogue*, forced himself to confront and conquer his most-hated foods (kimchi, anchovies, dill, swordfish, Indian desserts) before accepting the job.

"Maybe we could just eat something else," Rich said, and he'd turned on the hot water.

. . .

ACROSS LEXINGTON AVENUE, the double gold domes of the Central Synagogue are shimmering in the day's last half hour of light. By 5 P.M., the view from my dirty third-floor office window will be shortened to my own dark reflection, making me sit up straighter each time I look up.

"You need to get out of here," I tell my unhappy co-worker, Kay. "Life's too short." Her shared corner office is big and drafty, so she comes to my tiny office to warm up and complain that she has stayed longer at this job than she meant to. Which each of us is guilty of. The technology magazine we work for was purchased a year ago by a ninety-seven-year-old multimillionaire in Beverly Hills, who built his fortune on pool and spa magazines in the 1970s; he still goes into his Los Angeles office each morning, falls asleep at his desk after lunch, and occasionally calls us to make small, never-remotely-predictable comments about the table of contents, or the phrasing of a subtitle, in a hoarse, wonderfully rickety voice that it's the office pastime to imitate.

While each of us secretly toils toward the careers we wish we had, the physical office itself makes it an easy job to treat as a way station. There's no kitchen, no coffee; piles of mail are stacked in the entryway, since the receptionist was let go. Every corner that could be cut is now missing. Which made it still more ridiculous, this summer, that when we hunkered down in the conference room to hash out the next year's editorial calendar, someone had the gall to rob this place, cherry-picking items from our desktops and drawers. Security footage later showed a man in a dark-blue suit walking past the building's perennially drowsy doorman with a fuller backpack than he had arrived with. At the time, I was upset to be without my cellphone and wallet, but I had to laugh later, imagining our dapper thief shining his shoes, meticulously plotting the perfect caper, only to be rewarded with our ragtag suite: the rustling plastic taped to Kay's drafty windows; the piles of paper and plastic that Kay and I have determined to recycle ourselves, since the building isn't interested; the sallow walls and buzzing lights in the sales guy's asylum-like hovel; and the death-metal posters covering the walls of the editor in chief's office, creating the distinct feeling that there might also be *Playboy* magazines in the filing cabinet and dirty underwear and pizza crusts under the desk.

"What about you!" Kay says, lifting her face toward my

blowing ceiling vent and better stretching her full six feet under it. She's not in the mood for a hypocrite's pep talk.

Before this, before Columbia, I was working in Malibu. And I was in Los Angeles only because my sister Bridget and her husband, Wes, moved there, and then Maria went out for college, and my mother went out to be with her grandchildren, once Bridget started having them, and, not knowing what to do with myself after college, I went out, too. But still. *Malibu!* I had sunshine, permanent flip-flop weather, and the world's greatest commute: thirty easy minutes up the Pacific Coast Highway, with shimmering water, bobbing surfers, and celebrity mansions decoratively spread alongside me both ways. I had a raise and a promotion and an office that opened to a breezy patio with a view to the ocean on clear days. And after work, while the traffic thinned, there was the length of Zuma Beach to run, with the sun low on the water, the occasional silhouette of dolphin dorsal fins, and mothers with small children packing up beach toys. (And I had done so little to deserve these things, really, had more or less simply shown up!)

There was the smell of jasmine, and the farm stand selling local honey, and once, at the gas station before the ride back down the PCH, I saw two shooting stars in the time it took to fill the tank of my Honda. But I was working for a technology magazine, and I hated technology. And maybe even magazine publishing wasn't for me. Maybe I wanted to write books, or to teach, or to teach writing. I was twenty-four, and if I didn't begin to lay the groundwork for a career I actually wanted, I told myself, I'd be stuck in the wrong jobs forever. So I came up with the brilliant plan of graduate school, followed by the brilliant plan of borrowing a staggering sum of money—a sum it now seems indecent to let a person in pajamas, alone at her desk at 6 A.M., legally sign up for.

Now it's six months since I delivered my thesis, my loan payments are all coming due, and I'm at work on another technology magazine, in a room approximately the size of my bed.

I rub my forehead, turn back to my keyboard, and Kay reluctantly pulls in her legs and stands to leave. "I'm working on it," I tell her.

Commuting home, there are suddenly no L trains arriving at Union Square, and inside of ten minutes the platform fills to where my two default thoughts are a fear of someone being jostled onto the track and a surety that, were something to cause everyone to run for the stairs (a gunshot, a fire, or, my personal post–September 11 phobia, a swirl of poison gas), people would be crushed in the act. When the trains finally begin arriving again, three go by before I can press myself inside one, and once I do, I'm pinned between the bodies of strangers, unable even to reach for the *New Yorker* in my purse.

This job is all part of the plan! I reassure myself. I took the job the week I turned in my thesis because it was offered to me, and because I had twenty-three dollars in my checking account and the hours were nine to five—unheard of in Manhattan—which I thought would give me time to rework the essays in my thesis. If I can get a few of them into literary journals, I'm hoping to pitch the whole thing as a book. I wake up ninety minutes early each morning to sit and write before work, and Rich applauds my discipline, but it's a terrified desperation that propels me from the bed. I need to know that I'm not still living my old life, only now with less space and more debt.

The train lurches at a turn, and collectively we sway left

and then upright again, too tightly packed for individual movement. Still, I suck in to try making myself smaller, so that whatever body part of the person behind me is touching me, can be touching me less.

By the time I reach our front door, I'm sweating inside my winter coat. The deadbolt rolls back noisily, and I find Rich on the phone at the peninsula of kitchen counter, where he likes to work in his uniform of T-shirt, jeans, and ugly mustard bedroom slippers. He gives me a smile and a finger to the lips to show that he's recording an interview. Rich is an excellent fiction writer, despite not having come to it until his last year of college (dutiful Chinese son, his original major was aerospace engineering), but for now his bread and butter is writing about cars.

I decide to skip the gym and head back out to the grocery store, Pitts, where I find the rest of the neighborhood already in line. When I get back home Rich is off the phone, and he gives me a kiss and a hug, and, with an arm still around me, smoothes my hair around my ear.

"How's my baby?" he asks. I press my face into his T-shirt, and he puts both arms back around me and a kiss on the top of my head. "Do we need to free you from the bank?"

There's a bit we both like in *A Moveable Feast,* where Ezra Pound raises money so that T. S. Eliot can quit his job at a London bank and get back to the business of being a poet.

"Yeah, Citibank," I laugh, pulling away. It's the majority holder of my student loans. "My variable rate just went up."

Dinner tonight is a joint effort. I sauté matchstick-cut carrots with butter and cilantro, just because we have it, while

Rich makes himself a pork chop I ordered from FreshDirect, an online grocery-delivery service. The pescatarian is complimented on her meat-picking prowess. He deglazes the pan with the open red wine from two nights ago and adds a Bosc pear that I find in the refrigerator drawer and meant to eat with the blue cheese from a few nights ago. I also make my Aunt Teresa's zucchini quiche, the only recipe I know that calls for Bisquick, and that (along with breaded shrimp under the broiler, chocolate mousse to stand a spoon in, and a perfectly dressed romaine salad) instantly brings to mind my favorite aunt.

The meal is an odd smorgasbord, but there's a cozy sense of having accomplished something together. Rich lights the two votive candles I set the table with and pours the last inch of wine into our waiting glasses. There is more to open, but we both want to work tonight. Three sips apiece. For taste, he says.

We talk about the day we each had, the article he's working on, and then a friend who was told he has two ghosts in his apartment—which, absurdly, is my biggest fear. How can he sleep there?

"How come no one ever sees ghost dogs or ghost horses, only ghost people?" Rich wonders instead.

"Because dogs don't have souls."

"I bet people who love dogs think dogs have souls," he says.

Later, we turn to the greater mystery of how it is that, beyond his springtime proposal, we've done little toward actually getting married. "October," we first told people, which has turned into "Probably May." But now we're midway through January and, with the excuse of the holidays behind us, it is time to start planning this wedding.

I am the planner in this relationship—the one who re-members birthdays, makes grocery lists. In my desk at this very moment is a list of acquaintances I don't want to forget to invite to our next party, whenever that might be. But for maybe the first time, my hyper-organizing Virgo instincts are failing me. We haven't yet discussed a wedding budget, and I certainly have no extra money to make deposits with or to begin planning around, so these last few months I've felt as though I've been standing with one foot optimistically raised but no direction to put it down in.

There had also been the issue of my mother. While she liked Rich as a person, she didn't find him to be marrying ma-terial. She wanted me to marry a good Christian man I could trust in and lean on because he was trusting and leaning on Christ—the natural hierarchy of the Christian marriage. Surely she should have known that a proposal would come eventually; though I imagine she expected that I would break up with him before one did, since I'd said it was important to me to marry a Christian, as the Bible instructed. And once, actually, I almost had. I wrote Rich a long note explaining that I was afraid breaking up was the right thing to do, emailed it off, left for church with my mother and sister, and cried through the entire service. When I got home, Rich had emailed back saying that he couldn't open the version of Word I'd sent the note in—which was a relief to the degree that it felt more honest than what I'd written. What I believed I should want, and what I honestly wanted, it seemed, were separate things.

The weekend Rich proposed we'd flown to Los Angeles for our friends' Sunday wedding. Our six-year anniversary was that Saturday, and to celebrate we'd made reservations at our old favorite restaurant, an Italian place in a strip mall in the Valley. It had a garden across the street, where the owners grew zucchini flowers they stuffed and fried with the lightest hand (equaled, in my experience, only by my Aunt Diva, a native Tuscan), and a dining room run by a charming Belgian named Henri, who would exercise his French with Rich and tell us how, arriving in America forty years ago, he learned to speak English entirely by listening to the radio.

Before dinner, Rich had suggested a drive out to Malibu, where we found a quiet spot to sit and exchange anniversary gifts, and eventually he got down on one knee and proposed. (I expected the proposal was coming, but the knee I wasn't sure of.)

"Why don't we wait until we're back in New York to call everyone?" I'd suggested, admiring the most valuable thing I suddenly owned—had *ever* owned—brightly flashing on my left hand. I knew a friend who'd done this, savored the news between the two of them, and I liked the idea of it; but maybe a part of me also knew that my call wouldn't be met with all the enthusiasm I wanted to enjoy that night.

My mother loves my sisters and me with an intensity that can be overwhelming. "When you girls were babies, I'd kiss you until my lips were chapped!" she likes to tell us. No challenge I've ever approached has been too big or small for her to insist, out of the fullness of her love or ignorance, that I was the best at, the most right for, the most deserving of. Once, shortly after I'd moved to Los Angeles, I signed up to run a 5K. On the morning of the race she drove me, and there were road detours and we got lost, and as we pulled into the parking area the starting gun cracked. I hurried to the registration table, grabbed my number, and ran off still pinning it to my chest. That fall, I was working an unpaid magazine internship and waiting tables six days a week; I was far from my best friend, Erin, who had been with me through high school and college; and I'd recently discovered that the boy I'd met my senior year, and fully imagined myself marrying, was secretly also dating his ex-girlfriend. And so I took off running hard, fueled by the frustration of being late to the race and slowly graduating to the full litany of anxieties that can make a broke twenty-one-year-old feel helpless and horrible.

Soon I had passed all the walkers, and then the joggers, and eventually I was running with the runners, and in the last few hundred meters I spotted my mother in the fenced-off crowd, jumping and cheering and yelling something with my name. As I got closer, I realized she was screaming: "Punch it, Michelle! *Punch it!!!*" I think I laughed out loud. Where had she learned this funny thing to say? Still, encouraged, I passed four more runners before the chute; and still today, when I'm running alone and willing myself up a hill, I picture her up ahead on my right and I hear the words again in my ears: *Punch it!*

In the end, my mother learned of our engagement before I called, and for three months she wouldn't speak to me. It was a response so far off the charts of what I knew reality to be that those months were a sort of purgatory during which I half expected to wake from a crazy dream. "Does Rich hate Mom?" Bridget asked with concern, as slowly each of us grasped that our family was drifting farther from the norm than we'd ever imagined it.

"No, if anything, he says he feels bad for me," I told her. "He just thinks she's crazy." During these months I wavered between hurt, anger, and embarrassment. It was because of her that I'd conducted my love life so fastidiously as to border on the absurd; and yet, when the time finally came for me to choose, she was so sure I was making a mistake that she couldn't bear to speak to me.

"Is it because I'm Chinese?" Rich asked, shortly before we moved. We were sitting on the couch in his old apartment on the Upper West Side, him slumped into it and me perched on the cushion's edge.

"No, it's because you're not a good Christian," I told him, cringing to hear the words aloud. Who had the moral authority to say such things? "She thinks I'm going against God's will by marrying someone who's a less faithful Christian than I am, and she's terrified that by willingly putting myself farther from God I'm damning myself to hell for all eternity."

"I'm a Christian!" He tried to sound indignant.

"Not *really*," I said, beginning to feel irritated. "You never want to go to church. You believe in *energy*. . . . You totally tricked me when I met you. You said you were a Christian, and you told me that story about when you were in college, going to church every day with the old ladies for your Lenten penance."

"I *did* do that," he said. "And then I decided it was ridiculous. . . . And you tricked me, too! You came out wearing that Red Sox hat the first time we went hiking, and you said you'd seen Clemens pitch. I thought you knew about baseball. You don't know *anything* about baseball!"

I leaned back into the couch. "I said I liked the Red Sox. That is not the same as saying I know anything about baseball." He tugged at me so that I slumped toward him, and he put a kiss on my temple.

"Can we please just go to church on Sundays, so we both don't damn ourselves to hell?" I asked.

"Okay," he said, resigned.

"Promise?"

"I promise."

Around Thanksgiving my mother relented. She spent a long time talking with her pastor and finally concluded that, as painful as it was to watch, she had to let me make my own mistakes. I opted to ignore the insult in this and take what I could get; I wanted my mother back.

Which narrowed our wedding obstacles back down to money. I'm embarrassed to realize that, for all the time I waited for a ring, I barely considered the financial consequences that one would lead to. I was a student, barely managing to cover the rent; saving for a wedding wasn't an option. (And besides, what kind of girl would I have been, to be planning for a wedding before I'd even been proposed to!) Rich did well in his last job and left with a big bonus, but he had leaned on those savings in moving to New York and then building a freelance career here. And, I imagine, in buying the ring.

Part of me wishes that my parents had a secret stash of money waiting for this—while another part winces at the logic of wanting my parents to pay so that I can do this very grown-up thing. Though when Rich's parents generously offered to pay I was embarrassed by the unevenness of that, too. At some point we agreed we should just pay for the wedding ourselves, though the logistics of this have yet to be worked out.

Rich takes his last meted-out swallow of wine. "I'll just take on more jobs, and we can put that money toward the wedding," he says. But he's already working constantly; where will he find the time? I should take some freelance assignments, I think. But it's so time-consuming to make contacts and pitch ideas, and between my job and reworking my thesis how can I possibly sit in front of the computer any longer? And when? He's a freelance writer with contacts already in place; he turns down assignments as it is.

"Well," I say, scrambling for something of my own to contribute in light of this gallantry. "I could, um, take on part of your share of the household stuff. I could do the grocery shopping and the cooking, so that you have more time for assignments." And, like that, I volunteer myself for exactly the role I have been working my entire conscious life to avoid. I don't want to keep a household running at a steady hum and clean and cook for a husband who enters the kitchen when food is hot on the table. Modern, intelligent couples eliminate the need for a housewife by evenly dividing the chores. Don't they? I want to be an equal, to split chores down the middle, to abandon the old gender roles.

Alix Kates Shulman, the author of the feminist manifesto *Memoirs of an Ex-Prom Queen,* wrote an article in the 1970s about how she and her husband created a Marriage Agreement, a sort of informal contract with all domestic and parenting duties spelled out and assigned. Every time I read it my reflex is to think her poor husband is overloaded; I have to remind myself that he's only now just doing half. "Eventually, as the old roles and habits are replaced, we may be able to abandon the formality of our arrangement," Shulman wrote, "but for now the formality is imperative. Good intentions are simply not enough."

It makes sense that it would take something as radical as a

written contract to break the ideas that were cemented into us as we grew up. And now maybe I've set us further off course.

Getting ready for bed, I bring it up again. "You know, this is kind of a dangerous precedent to be setting at the start of our marriage—you working all the time and me doing all the cooking," I say, toothbrush in hand, stepping out of the bathroom to look at him where he's writing. "We have to stay alert to the fact that this is a *temporary* situation, because at this impressionable stage patterns can be set that could affect the rest of our marriage. We are a team, and I am making a particular contribution, and you are making a particular contribution, and this is all very temporary. Right?"

"Right." Rich nods. "Of course."

APPLE CAKE

> 5 to 7 apples (using different types is ideal),
>   yielding about 4 cups when sliced or
>   cubed to about the size of grapes
> 1½ cups sugar (I've reduced this from the
>   2 cups my mother's recipe calls for; if
>   you like a sweeter cake, and you're not
>   the guilty type, go ahead and add an
>   extra half cup.)
> 2 cups flour
> 1¼ teaspoons baking soda
> 1 teaspoon cinnamon
> ½ teaspoon salt

2 large eggs, well beaten
½ cup vegetable oil
1 teaspoon vanilla extract

PREHEAT THE OVEN TO 325 DEGREES and grease your pan of choice. I like to use nonstick spray (which is probably killing us all gently, with whatever is in that can) and an 11 x 7-inch clear Pyrex dish because it's nice to be able to see when the sides become a deep caramel-brown and pull away from the pan.

Mix the dry ingredients in a very big bowl. Then set that aside and peel and chop the apples, leaving them on the cutting board or in the measuring cup if you bother to measure them; they just need to loiter somewhere for a moment.

In a second, smaller bowl, beat the eggs, then stir in the other wet ingredients.

Make a well in the center of the dry ingredients, pour in the wet ingredients, and mix until *just* combined. (It will seem, at first, that there's too much dry stuff, but eventually it works itself out.) Gently fold in the apples. The batter will become slightly more wet and manageable as you do this.

Bake for 45 minutes, or until a toothpick comes out cleanish and the cake is pulling away from the sides of the dish. Let it cool for about 20 minutes before serving in good-sized squares. As with so much in life, whipped cream or vanilla ice cream only makes this better.

ALTERNATE ROUTE

Another approach to this recipe, if you have a food processor and don't mind washing it, is to mix the dry ingredients in a big bowl, as described above. Then peel and chop *half* the apples and leave the other half cut into quarters. Put the quartered apples in the food processor and pulse a few times until they're the consistency of chunky applesauce. Then add the wet ingredients to the food processor and pulse until blended but not liquefied (a little texture is good). Make a well in the center of the dry ingredients, pour in the apple mixture, and mix until *just* combined. (This batter will be a lot wetter and more traditional than the one above.) Fold in the remaining apples. Baking instructions stay the same. This yields a cake with a different texture that I think is also worth trying.

PASTA WITH BROCCOLI RABE

> 1 head fresh broccoli rabe (no droopiness or
> blackened florets, please)
> Olive oil
> Garlic
> Red-pepper flakes
> Cheese for grating (Parmesan, Pecorino,
> Romano, or something similar)
> Salt and pepper
> Your pasta of choice; half a pound will serve two

PUT ON A BIG POT of salted water to boil for the
pasta. While you're waiting for it to boil, wash the
broccoli rabe, as you would normal broccoli. Breaking it down into bite-size pieces at this point will
make it easier to eat later, and I add it to the colander
in the sink as I go. The flowers, the leaves, and the
stalks can all be eaten, though take care to peel the
thick bottom stalk with a paring knife, using only its
more tender parts.

Once the water is boiling, drop in the broccoli
rabe for 60 seconds. Using a slotted spoon, lift it out
and lay it on a clean dishtowel to dry off for a minute.

Put the pasta into the pot of water once it has returned to a boil, and in a large frying pan heat 3 tablespoons of olive oil. When the oil is gently warmed,
add some finely chopped garlic—about 3 to 6 bulbs,
according to your preference. Let the garlic heat up
but not color, and keep the flame medium-low; you
don't want the garlic to burn when you add the broccoli rabe and any of its clinging water reacts with the
oil. (Another method is to heat the oil with the pepper flakes and two halved cloves of garlic, to give off
their flavor; then remove the cloves and throw them
away, add the broccoli rabe, and, once things have
calmed down, add the chopped garlic.)

With a wooden spoon, sauté the broccoli rabe
over medium heat. I find that it cooks in almost the
same amount of time as thin spaghetti. If things seem
to get dry, add more olive oil, or a splash of the pasta
water to keep things moist and simmering. I like broccoli rabe bright green and still slightly firm, and when

it's nearly there, if the pasta isn't ready yet, I'll turn off the heat under the broccoli rabe. Rich has drilled into my head: *The pasta waits for nobody!* Always let your sauce be waiting for the pasta, never the reverse.

When the pasta is about 30 seconds from your version of al dente, put the heat back on under the broccoli rabe, lift the pasta out of the water with tongs, and put it in the pan with the broccoli rabe. Drizzle more olive oil over it, grate a generous shaving of cheese over the top, toss the whole thing through in the pan, and serve with another grating of cheese. For extra flavor, you can also sprinkle in a quarter cup of bread crumbs at the end with the cheese.

Another dish, for when the cupboard seems truly bare, is *pasta aglio e olio*—pasta with garlic and oil—which is all of the above minus the broccoli rabe: al-dente pasta goes into a hot skillet with olive oil, garlic, red-pepper flakes, and a handful each of bread crumbs and cheese. Parsley or basil can also go in at the last moment. A bowl of this before bed, after a night of drinking, and you can laugh in the face of a hangover (all the way to the gym the next morning).

AUNT TERESA'S ZUCCHINI QUICHE

*4 cups zucchini, quartered lengthwise and
then sliced into small triangles. (If the
zucchini are large, slice them into eighths*

*instead. The goal is a triangle that will
be delicate in the mouth, not far from the
size of a corn kernel.)*

1 cup Bisquick
½ cup grated Parmesan or Romano cheese
1 small yellow onion, finely chopped
1 teaspoon parsley flakes
½ teaspoon basil or marjoram
¼ teaspoon salt
¼ teaspoon black pepper
4 large eggs, beaten
½ cup vegetable oil

HEAT THE OVEN TO 325 DEGREES. Combine
the dry ingredients, add the wet ones and the dry sea-
sonings, and mix until just combined. Pour into a
buttered pie tin or quiche dish and bake for 45 minutes, or until it's golden brown on top.

My aunt likes to make several quiches at once,
use disposable aluminum pie pans, and freeze them
prebaked; when she needs one, she lets it defrost in
the refrigerator before baking it. The trick to this, she
tells me, is to make them on a day when the freezer
is empty, so you can spread the pie pans out; if you
stack them before the batter is frozen, it'll squish out.

CHAPTER 3
Chineseification

WE HAVE AN EASY SATURDAY MORNING, READING THE newspaper with scrambled eggs, thick toast, and Americanos. Each time I tamp down the ground beans, I'm reminded of my father, after a late Sunday lunch, asking me to make him an espresso. "This way you'll know how to make it for your husband," he liked to say, enjoying the rustle of feminist indignation such teasing reliably provoked in his daughters. I was ten or eleven years old, and the espresso pot was a three-shot stovetop maker, more boxy than a Bialetti. I knew to pour it carefully and add the splash of anisette that he liked. "Yeah, right . . ." I'd grumble. "I'm *never* marrying an Italian." In the end, we were both right.

"I have such a taste for *rice cake*," Rich says suddenly, letting the word hang between us until its yeasty scent is in our noses and its porous, wet texture on our tongues. I was first introduced to Chinese rice cake in Los Angeles, at the drab downtown bakery Rich liked to visit before we stood in the inevitable line outside a popular dim-sum palace (red dragons, triple-height columns, hostesses in mandarin-collared dresses). The rice cakes were stiff, gummy white triangles that smacked of white vinegar, and their appeal was entirely lost on me; though Rich's enthusiasm for them was so great that each time I'd eventually take a bite. It wasn't until he moved to New York that I realized rice cake wasn't such an acquired taste after all, and that Los Angeles bakery was just selling stale, awful batches. Good rice cake, still warm, has a subtle yeasty aroma that's almost an almond essence, and the wriggly bounce of something steamed in a water bath. You can tear open a white triangle and see its airy, honeycomb-like chambers.

"Want to go to Chinatown for groceries?" he asks, knowing the bait is well set. I glance at the time: 10:50. If we leave any later, a Chinatown expedition will swallow the day entirely. We agree to skip showers, dress quickly, and head out.

The writer Calvin Trillin, a great lover of Chinatowns, once understandably lamented, "What may actually be my favorite dish in a number of Chinatown restaurants is something I have never even had the opportunity to taste, simply because of my inability to read the wall signs that announce some house specialties in Chinese." That such insider offerings might someday be made available to me was a possibility I first glimpsed the night I met Rich's parents. They were visiting Los Angeles for meetings his father had at UCLA, and they arranged to pick us up and take us to dinner.

"Shouldn't we pick *them* up?" I'd asked Rich, remembering how my heart had pounded on the 405 Freeway my first weeks in Los Angeles, and the ease with which I got myself lost. But Rich was unfazed. "They're pretty competent," he assured me, and sure enough they were curbside with ten minutes to spare, his father quiet but smiling in a jaunty light-blue driving cap, and his mother sparrow-thin, perfectly put together, and looking twenty years younger than I expected.

They met in Virginia as adults but had similar childhoods in China, where they were both born into wealthy families and later made to flee the Japanese and then the Communists. His mother's family had fled with a chef and a nanny in tow. Staying ahead of the occupation, the nanny would meet the children at the schoolroom door and they would travel for days, sleeping wherever they could and finally setting up somewhere new and invariably temporary. Eventually both families, unknown to the other, wound up in Taiwan. Years later, Rich's mother won a scholarship to attend Virginia Tech, and a friend of hers said that her older brother taught there; when she arrived and looked him up, she found a handsome, young full professor of physics, who also fenced and gave dancing lessons at the Fred Astaire school. During the second year of their marriage, he bought her a convertible green Triumph that Rich still marvels over. "What must people have thought, in the 1960s, about these two Chinese people driving around the Black Hills of Virginia in a British sports car?"

The night of that dinner, though, I knew little more about them than that his father was a genius physicist and his mother was responsible for his encyclopedic knowledge of black-and-white films. (I've never met another twenty-six-year-old who can identify Carole Lombard, Lana Turner, and Clifton Webb on sight.) We went to a cavernous Chinese restaurant in a crowded shopping strip in Monterey Park, a very Asian suburb of Los Angeles, and I deferred the ordering to the three of them, which they did in Mandarin. We ate well, and the conversation seemed to go smoothly, and though I was working hard to make a good impression, my confidence was buoyed by the navy blue dress I had bought for the occasion, imagining it the right combination of serious and pretty that would impress Chinese parents. Eventually our plates were cleared, and the meal seemed to be coming to a successful close. But then, with a dramatic, steam-billowing march across the dining room, held high overhead by a waiter in a limp black vest and rolled shirt-sleeves, the pièce de résistance arrived at our table: a whole broiled redfish, long as my arm.

It was probably the seven-thousandth whole fish of Rich's life, and he now makes something similar, though smaller, for us at home, but at the time I had never been served such a thing and it made an impression. Swift and agile, our waiter went to work with two serving spoons, and in no time he had bathed the fish a last time in its juices, deboned it, divided it four ways onto fresh plates, and topped each portion with a decorative arrangement of the ginger slices and scallion stalks that had made our fish seem so at home on his platter before those two flashing spoons had undone him.

That Rich's and my ethnic backgrounds are resources that we can draw on and share with each other is a point I appreciate now, though back then they hadn't seemed much more than aesthetics. With the arrival of that big redfish, however, it was clear that Rich had upped the ante on what it was he brought to the relationship.

Thanks to Rich, Chinatowns have also opened themselves to me. I've lost the old self-consciousness I used to feel, and now, emboldened, I'll sometimes practice a thank-you in Mandarin, which sounds to me like *Shey, shey!* This is usually met with dismissive nods, though an amused vendor once responded at some length and I could only smile and blush, having exhausted my shopping vocabulary. *"Ta tsai xiue,"* Rich told him. "She's still learning."

My entire phonetic grasp of the language currently extends to *Ch fan le* ("Time for dinner"); *Bu ke chi* (something close to "Don't be formal," which is used in place of "You're welcome," which the Chinese, like the Japanese, are too modest to say, as it would acknowledge that they've done something worth being thanked for); *Gon xi fa chai!* (Happy New Year!); and *Ni hao, bu hao?* (How are you?). Or, literally, "Good, not good?" In Mandarin, all questions are this efficient, offering no extra words, only the options for answers. To the ear, it's like a mallet being drawn across a xylophone and back the other way: Far, not far? Nice, not nice?

To complete my Chineseification (my sister Maria's word, after my hypercurly hair inexplicably smoothed itself out during my first year with Rich; my sister Bridget also experienced a hair-texture change around twenty-three, but hers was chalked up to a side effect of her first pregnancy), I occasionally also find myself craving Chinese rice cake. It's hardly sweet at all, but with black or green tea it's somehow a perfect snack.

At Canal Street we spill out of the Q train with the crowds and head to our usual places. First the long, skinny shop for a bag of frozen pork dumplings for him and frozen shrimp dumplings for me, and then the small steamy shop where there are always too many men behind the counter for the rice cake. It's sold here in flat plastic containers secured with a rubber band, since the rice cake is heavy and slippery and the container top constantly threatens to split and pop open.

Other places sell it in clear plastic sleeves that demand long tongs and deft maneuvering from the bakery worker, or else foam containers stapled shut; once the staple is out, though, the container never properly closes again, leaving any left-over rice cakes to dry out. It seems a fortune is waiting for the inventor of the perfect rice-cake container.

Since at just seventy-five cents it's too tempting to pass up, we also leave with two Styrofoam cups of *dofu wa,* the cus-tardlike tofu with a warm sugar syrup, which we eat standing on the slot of sidewalk between the parked cars and the streams of pedestrians. For Rich, *dofu wa* is a classic comfort food. He makes it each time we visit his parents, using the soft, fresh tofu that his mother buys in Boston's Chinatown in anticipation of our visit. On our first full afternoon in their quiet house, he'll pad down to the kitchen, pull out the yogurt-style container from behind bulging orange bags of Chinatown produce, and, with a flat serrated spoon like a bear paw, skim the tofu into thin white sheets. Then he sim-mers a simple syrup of sugar, water, and ginger slices in a small saucepan on the stove. In the time it takes the sugar to harden and then re-liquefy, his mother will stand at his shoul-der and talk excitedly about a movie she saw, or a trip she took, or the correct way to say something in Mandarin and why the tidy phrasing makes perfect sense. His sisters, also home for the holiday, will gradually put down their books or instruments or laptops and emerge from their bedrooms. And, hearing them congregate, his father, still keeping his head warm with some version of that first British driving cap, will shuffle from his office to the kitchen with a growing smile, never failing to be delighted by the sight of his three grown children.

When the syrup is finally amber and bubbling, Rich will announce that it's ready, six white bowls of thin tofu sheets will be lined up at the counter's edge, and the five of us will lean in to watch him gingerly flood each stack. Then the last strains of winter sun will leak into the kitchen, which has changed little since these siblings walked the trail from their wooded backyard to the nearby elementary school, and for the next few minutes the only sounds are of our ceramic spoons tapping the insides of our bowls as we tip them back and forth, flooding each spoonful of tofu with the warm sugar syrup.

Disposing of our sticky *dofu-wa* cups, we turn up Mulberry Street and, at the tiered wooden stalls attached to a convenience store, buy garlic, scallions, bok choy, Chinese broccoli, and a comically large bundle of yard-long beans—a longer, tougher-skinned cousin of the American string bean that, secured with a large rubber band, looks like a ponytail of dreadlocks. From there we stop at the second seafood shop on the street and choose from its fish laid out on ice alongside the buckets of shrimp, crabs, and crawfish that extend onto the sidewalk. Insisting that he still has a free hand, Rich then heads to the butcher shop two doors up for a container of marinated pork ribs, and I visit the bakery next door for the two-for-a-dollar, cupcake-size egg custards packaged in sturdy aluminum tins that keep their flaky crusts from breaking.

We arrange the fish against the frozen dumplings to keep them cool, redistribute the bags between us, and, fully loaded down, head back to the subway. We maneuver around the crowds walking to restaurants and spilling out of restaurants, past sidewalk vendors with folding tables piled with a single offering (garlic, pomegranates) or else long cornucopias of lychees, clusters of brown longans still on their stems, hairy red rambutans with their sea-urchin looks, and bright fuchsia dragon fruits, with a sample sliced open to show its startling white flesh and black polka dots. We pass tourists buying lucky bamboo stalks, paper banners with their names hand-painted in kitschy letters, and big green coconuts that men with machetes have shaped to look like tropical cocktails, complete with bent straws. Silver-dollar-size turtles paw determinedly at the walls of Tupperware cages outside trinket shops, and somber locals crowd around silver street carts serving hot beef strips or fried noodles straight from their searing cooktops. And, as always, there are people of every race and age browsing and shopping and entering and leaving the entrances of open storefronts displaying knockoff handbags and wristwatches, packaged perfumes, rainbows of pashminas, shiny hair clips and combs, tea sets, back scratchers, chopsticks, soup spoons, flip-flops, jade pendants, paper parasols, Buddha statues with water features, and endless key chains, T-shirts, and mugs. Down in the subway, we transfer from the Q to the L train, glad for the single flight of stairs, and within an hour of making it home each of us needs a nap. And the day is done.

Today we bought shrimp still in their shells, two large cod fillets, two halibut fillets, a pound of squid (mostly because, at $2.99, we couldn't resist it), and a plastic container of oysters in their liquor. It's about eight ounces for five dollars, which would have been frighteningly cheap elsewhere but in China-town seemed a legitimate bargain. Rich hesitated at first, frowning at the clear container and its goopy contents, but the fishmonger encouraged us to dredge them in cornmeal and fry them, and, having just finished M.F.K. Fisher's *Consider the Oyster*, I excitedly rattled off more possibilities—oysters Rockefeller, oyster soup, oyster bisque, oysters with noodles—and he was swayed.

After some deliberation, we put the cod and the halibut in the freezer and the oysters, shrimp, and squid in the refrigerator—a big decision in a household where defrosted ground beef is treated like a ticking bomb. Of the three, the squid seems the most time-sensitive, so around dinnertime, the day having gone dark hours ago, I search *The Gourmet Cookbook* for squid recipes. Then Rich calls his mother and I call mine, and in the end we settle on some combination of their similar methods.

Rich rinses the slippery white bodies, carefully extracts the single, quill-like bone, slices them into rings, sautés them with garlic, scallions, red-pepper flakes, and a splash of ice-cold vodka for fifty seconds, and we eat them alongside rice and the bok choy I sautéed in garlic and ginger. The squid could have used some ginger as well, but it was good enough, and in the end it was dinner for two with multiple food groups for approximately four dollars. Which, as two people saving money, we do much congratulating each other about.

Before bed, our stomachs tugging at us again, I split a large, floppy rice cake triangle between two dessert plates and brew two cups of jasmine tea, dropping three hard, shriveled jasmine leaves into each of our mugs. In their glass jar in the cupboard, the dark, misshapen pieces could be a collection of dead flies, but in the steaming water they languidly unfurl, showing their color to be actually more khaki, and come to sway at the bottoms of the mugs like soft sea grass. Rich joins me at the peninsula of countertop, and we stand eating by the dim light of the end-table lamp. He hums happily, barely consciously, the way the Matt Dillon character in *The Flamingo Kid* did all those years ago. But at least this covers the smushy sound of the rice cakes, which is like eating overripe bananas.

...

"AN OYSTER LEADS a dreadful but exciting life," *Consider the Oyster* begins. From there it details the travails faced by the hundreds of millions of eggs released by a single adult oyster over a balmy summer, making it seem miraculous any make it to our plates at all. Enamored of M.F.K.'s descriptions of delicately curling oyster edges in soups and bisques and stews, "mildly potent, quietly sustaining, warm as love and welcomer in winter," I decide to simmer the oysters in a light broth that Rich is adept at creating from some combination of the dark bottles that live in the cabinet above the stove—soy sauce, sesame oil, oyster sauce, fish sauce, and various vinegars—and serve them with bok choy and udon noodles.

When the soup is ready, I ladle it into deep white bowls that emit satisfying, photogenic steam clouds. The broth has a slight glisten, and the noodles look hearty beside the green ribbons of bok choy. But then there are the oysters, big sloppy gray ovals, like half-full sacks of toys. A male organ comes to mind.

"I guess I should have cut them up," I say, nudging one with my chopsticks.

Rich stares into his bowl for a long moment, the anti-Narcissus squinting past the soup's surface. Then he cinches an oyster between his chopsticks, resolutely chews and swallows, and finally blows out several quick breaths, as though he's just completed an athletic event. "So, yeah . . ." he says slowly, nodding a little to confirm this to himself. "I can't eat these."

I eat two. The first to see for myself and the second out of guilt over wasting food. There's a restaurant up the street that sells oysters on the half shell that are petite and metallic and go down in one light swallow that leaves the mouth feeling bright and effervescent and the swallower as though she's had a day at the beach. But these monsters fill the whole mouth disgustingly and then require chewing. We each finish our noodles and bok choy and leave the gray sacks sitting heavily below the broth line in our bowls.

I admit that I've imagined a version of my future wifely self who can reliably whip up a few key dishes when the moment demands. The boyfriend of a girl I once briefly lived with told me that he traveled with the girl's family to a far-off rental house one summer, and when they finally arrived, exhausted and famished, the girl's mother quickly put together a pan of corn pudding that was just about the best thing he'd ever eaten. He told me this while waiting for a pan of it to cool on my stovetop. The corn-pudding recipe was the one good thing I got out of that sublet, and the fact that it has only five ingredients in no way lessens my delight in it—or my respect for a woman who's willing to travel with creamed corn in her luggage. Like her, I can now reliably deliver a corn pudding in a pinch, though topping my wish list are a first-rate piecrust, perfect buttermilk biscuits, and a high, moist crumbly corn bread. Oysters, though . . . I decide I won't mind if I never master the oyster.

I tip the dregs from our bowls into the trash and tie up the bag, while Rich puts on his coat to deliver it to the curb. He gives me a kiss at the handoff and says, with the panache of a secret agent off to destroy the evidence, "Let's never speak of this again."

. . .

THE LAST SUNDAY in late January is damp and raw, and we get home long past dark from a day in New Jersey at my sister Bridget's house. Traffic was backed up for an hour on the New Jersey side of the Holland Tunnel, Rich's allergies were in high gear, and as we entered the traffic he ran out of tissues. Then we had to drop the rental car off in the city and wait on the cold platform for the subway, which on a Sunday evening was in no hurry to arrive. When we finally reach our front door, I'm so hungry, cold, and miserable, I can't decide whether to take a hot shower or just lie on the floor and cry.

Rich wants to order in, but because it's faster he eventually agrees to bowls of our respective boiled dumplings, which we eat with a side of Chinese broccoli that I sauté, while the dumplings boil, with garlic, red-pepper flakes, and a few drips of purple-black oyster sauce.

Freezing rain fell most of the day, and we'd sat with Bridget and Wes looking out their patio doors, past the water-logged deck with its piles of gray melting snow, past the in-ground pool with its cover sagging under the weight of dead leaves and blown children's toys, and beyond the scraggly grasses encircling the drab, brown pond, whose geese have abandoned it for God only knows, to where the property's long back lawn was muddy and dull. And then we agreed to have the wedding there.

The four of us strained to imagine a white tent set back on a stretch of green lawn. "We'll fertilize all spring!" By May, Bridget assured us, the bare trees around the property will be a lush forest, the pond will have a ring of downy grass around it, the white geese will have a peeping gaggle, peonies the size of soccer balls will be in bloom around the pool—"We'll float candles in the water!"—and fleets of purple irises will stand rows deep around the perimeter of the house. We imagined stringing twinkle lights inside the tent, and putting white candles in Mason jars on the rickety wooden fence posts encircling the property.

After more than a decade in Los Angeles, they've moved back to New Jersey to be close to family, but now Bridget is depressed by the gray and the cold and feeling daunted by this house that they and their three young children have moved into. Clearly it will someday be magnificent, but right now it's in need of an incredible amount of work. The hundreds of perennial bulbs waiting under the graying snow are the one positive legacy left by the past owner, who was ill and abandoned the house in the end.

Rich and I both like the idea of a casual wedding "at home," and it'll definitely be less expensive to have the wedding there. When I called a few Long Island vineyards to check prices, many of them charged a five-thousand-dollar site fee before anything was even rented. We also like that the party could take its natural course, and at midnight the lights won't be turned up by a tired waitstaff. Plus, Bridget insists, the deadline of the wedding will help keep their planned renovations on schedule. A country lane curves around the back of the house (I've never described anything as a country lane before, but if such a thing exists it's this road), where guests could park and walk directly up to the tent, and there's even a pretty white church nearby, with a nice woman pastor.

"It's amazing of you to offer, but it's too much," Rich had said. "And the kids . . ." he trailed off. "It would be way too much work. It would be unfair to you."

No, no, no, they said. We'd love to host. It would be so much fun.

"You will *hate* us by the time it's over," I told Bridget gravely. "It will be way more work than you expect, and you'll wind up regretting that you offered."

What's the big deal? There'll be a tent, a caterer. Everything will be taken care of. It'll be perfect, they insisted.

Their one small concern was for the house's old septic tank, so in the end we agreed to keep it small. Fifty guests—never mind that I have forty-one first cousins—for a spring wedding. "May, not June," was my one request. I've always been the warm-blooded person who's sweating when everyone else is comfortable; the last thing I want is to be zipped into satin under a ninety-degree sun. Though the weather in this part of the country is so erratic, absolutely anything is possible.

Our stomachs full and the crankiness drained from us, I download an almanac to check its weather predictions. In college I had a friend from Maine with a charming father who wrote for the almanac, and while he admitted little about its accuracy, my adoration for the friend has since attached itself to the book. We choose a date: May 14, seven days before our seven-year dating anniversary. Are sevens lucky? I hope so.

DOFU WA

> *Very soft dofu-wa-style tofu (in the container,*
>   *it looks more like yogurt than traditional*
>   *tofu)*
> *1 cup white sugar*
> *1 cup water*
> *Half a thumb of ginger, sliced into rounds*

SKIM THE SOFT TOFU into thin sheets with a big spoon, layering as much as you'd like into a bowl. Six ounces for each person is usually about right.

Put the sugar into a saucepan and stir it over medium heat. It will melt and liquefy and turn an increasingly dark caramel color. Cook it until it's very dark brown, nearly burnt. Then, with a lid ready, pour in the water and quickly cover the pot, as this will instantly splatter everywhere. (It should be said that this is Rich's recipe, and other chefs perhaps do this differently and more safely.) Once the craziest part of the splattering has subsided, reduce the heat and stir the sugar until it dissolves entirely. Add the sliced ginger, stirring for another minute, so it imparts its flavor. Pour this over each bowl of tofu, holding back the ginger slices with a wooden spoon.

CHAPTER 4

February

...

WHEN THE WRITER M.F.K. FISHER SET SAIL FOR FRANCE in 1929, she was young, beautiful, and had been married for just a week. Her new husband, Al, was finishing his doctorate in Dijon, and when they arrived he settled into his course work while she searched out a home for them, eventually securing a room in a classic Burgundian town house across from the archbishop's garden. Their rent included meals, three a day, which they sat to at their host family's table. When I try to imagine what the beginnings of a marriage should look like, M.F.K. is always my first thought.

I take down my favorite mixing bowl, a blue-and-white polka-dot number that began its useful life in my maternal grandmother's kitchen, and beat together two eggs, ricotta, salt, pepper, dried parsley, and about a half cup of Parmesan, grating it directly into the bowl. *We are setting up house,* I say to myself, trying to make it feel real. *This will be our marital home.*

M.F.K. (I've read that she preferred to be called Mary Frances, but as ours has long been a relationship on the page it's difficult to think of her by anything but these initials) and Al were boarders in that town house for two years, until the desire for a home of their own finally gripped them and they left for a studio above a pastry shop with floor-to-ceiling windows, the aroma of peach tarts pushing through the floor, and a street address that their more polite acquaintances refused to visit.

It makes little sense, really, that this is where my mind's eye should go—by that point they were already two years into their marriage, and it actually lasted only a handful more—but this is the part my brain clicks to: the setting up and settling in. It was the first-ever day-to-day cooking for this woman who would go on to become a doyenne of gastronomy and the century's finest food writer, and it wasn't until she settled into that apartment that she first began to think about what to serve and how to eat and who she wanted at her table, which were ideas that would define her and her work into the next century. Which I guess better explains why I return again and again to the image of her in that studio, taking her first steps down what would be a long, wonderful path: it's not the beginnings of her marriage, after all, but of her finding herself.

Of her first week in that studio she later wrote: "It was the longest, most discouraging, most exciting and satisfying week I could remember, and I look back on it now with an envy that is no less real for being nostalgic. I do not think I could or would ever do it again; I am too old. But then, in the town I loved and with the man I loved, it was fine."

I slide half a box of lasagna noodles into a pot of salted water, now at a strenuous boil, and drizzle in olive oil after them. Lasagna, for me, is no sure thing. Sometimes, whether in roll form or the traditional way, it turns out great: the filling thickens and the whole thing is moist and succulent, if

that word can be used in a non-meat context. And then sometimes it's sort of deflated, and the pasta is dry, and it's a little
depressing considering the time involved and the investment
of the ricotta. My success seems to hinge, I'm realizing, on
the amount of sauce on the bottom of the pan and spooned
over the finished product, and, to a lesser extent, the number
and size of the eggs. Too much tomato anything, though,
and Rich will be curled on the sofa with a stomachache, so I
pour just a half cup of sauce into the bottom of a white baking dish and shake it until it's evenly distributed.

There's a block of chopped spinach in the freezer, so I put it
in the microwave until it's warm but still filled with enough icy
shards that I can handle it. Then I put the green mess into the
center of a clean dishtowel and wring it over the sink until all the
liquid runs out. Whoever told me to do this had called it a tea
towel, which I liked, and squeezing the spinach now, my mind
fingers the words again, *tea towel, tea towel,* which then reminds
me of the Robert Hass poem I kept in my car's clean ashtray the
year I moved to Los Angeles, to distract myself in heavy traffic:
"Such tenderness, those afternoons and evenings, / saying
blackberry, blackberry, blackberry."

I drain the lasagna noodles in the silver colander and then
wash, dry, and flatten a few basil leaves into a neat stack before rolling them cigar style to cut in a chiffonade, the way
I've seen it done on TV. But their scent is almost tangible, and
I can't resist walking the small bouquet to Rich where he's
working at the kitchen table and saying, "Smell." He sniffs it,
smiles, and turns back to his laptop—a gesture entirely to appease me. He is the son of a scientist, and we both know his
default thought is of the thousands of plant-dwelling micro-
organisms that fly into the nose with each inhale.

I put the leaves to my nose again, thinking their scent the essence of *green* and wonder at what stale reflexes some memories are. That I can't stand over the mixing bowl without the feeling of standing on a chair beside my mother, shaking parsley flakes onto a clean white mound of ricotta with painstaking slowness (so that for one minute, at least, no one could accuse me of being too impatient and careless), and my mother eyeing it and encouraging, "A little more, a little more . . ."

Will the smell of basil ever not instantly conjure my childhood backyard, the flash of verdant, late-summer garden, lovely but so predictable? I'm sure it's an association informed by a hundred small moments, but it brings me to one particular evening with the light fading in our hedge-lined yard; my father standing with the unraveled hose, watering the garden we planted together; the warm scents of the basil and tomato leaves rising up under the cool spray; and the water in our little pool rhythmically sloshing in response to the filter's drawbridge mouth dropping open and slowly closing again. And all of this turning around my mother, sitting on the back-porch steps with a bolt of clover-green felt, relining the collection baskets from our church.

It was a task she had initiated, after weeks of noting their disintegrating interiors, and finally she had approached the priests about it. They told her the baskets would need to be back in time for the 6 A.M. mass, maybe wishing to discourage the hassle, but my mother was undaunted. She drove to a fabric store while the baskets were emptied of their noon-service tithes, and when she pulled back into the church parking lot, two priests—one of them ever so slightly pausing, midway, in perhaps a fuller consideration of what it was they were doing—loaded the stacked baskets into the deep trunk of her silver Cadillac. When I joined her on the porch steps that evening, she had been cutting and pasting green felt circles into the creaky, glazed-straw baskets for hours. The scoop neck of her T-shirt showed the light freckles on her chest, and her dirty-blond hair was arranged in a small ponytail high on her head. My older cousins liked to say that she looked like Barbara Eden in *I Dream of Jeannie,* and with her hair up like this she especially did.

Whether I care to recall it all or not, the basil conjures and the brain delivers: the warm garden, the indigo dusk, the safe enclosure of the yard, my awe at having such sacred church objects stacked on my own back porch, and the feel of being so in love with my mother, who was sweet and kind and pretty. It was shortly afterward that she became born again and we left that church; she asked Jesus to come into her life and show her what to do, and he did, and nothing has been the same since.

I break up the dried spinach and add it to the ricotta batter along with more salt, ground pepper, a pinch of nutmeg, and the thin ribbons of basil, and then spread the mixture down the centers of eight somewhat cooled lasagna noodles, rolling them gently so their fillings stay inside. The finished rolls, with their spiraling green interiors and little fluted edges all pointed north, are pretty in the white casserole, with its thin layers of red sauce on top and below. I cover the dish with foil, slide it into the refrigerator, change into gym clothes, and leave Rich with instructions so that he's pulling it out of the oven as I'm walking back through the door. Then I walk the three blocks to the gym without headphones, still dragging my family along beside me.

...

OUR FRIENDS JAMES and Allison were married last fall in the Berkshires, the mountains due west of Boston. We headed up in a bright-yellow car Rich was given to test-drive, and which we both felt sure would earn us a ticket, and before we were across the New York State border, the best of the foliage still ahead of us, we had one. The wedding site was an artists' retreat, and its empty bungalows were offered to overnight guests. There was a clearing in the woods for the ceremony—the bride with tiny pink flowers in her long, wild hair; felled tree trunks arranged as pews; and the invocation of an Amish tradition in which, unless moved to talk, we all simply sat silently, filling our noses with the clear pine air, smiling at one another and absorbing the view of our hosts and the whole world behind them: a gold-and-green valley and then mountains, mountains, mountains. During the cocktail hour, we happily crunched down the gravel paths that wound around the property and found our names and table numbers adorably strung on makeshift clotheslines. Dinner was under a white tent, and the dancing went long into the night, in a red barn with a well-stocked iTunes playlist and a bar. In simplicity, scale, and sentiment, we loved it all and agreed that we'd like something similar. So we were shocked to later learn it had cost them eighteen thousand dollars.

"But Allison made the invitations herself," I told Rich.

"And James said the site fee was only five hundred dollars—that there'd never been a wedding there before," he marveled back. So what added up to eighteen thousand dollars?

My friend Erin, laughing when I repeat this to her, sends me the itemized master list from her wedding, a daunting

142 items that she dragged from TO DO to DONE columns. I move "Get premarital blood work" to DONE, since it's not required in New Jersey, and close the overwhelming document.

"What do you want to eat?"

"I don't know, what do you want to eat?"

For ten minutes we peer into cabinets and open and close the refrigerator. Finally, Rich excavates a deli container of Kalamatas from the second shelf of the refrigerator, and we agree on bucatini with tuna, done the way Patrik taught me, which is essentially a puttanesca. Just a sautéed onion, some capers or olives, red-pepper flakes, a can of chopped tomatoes, and a drained can of tuna. The cooked pasta is tossed through the sauce with another splash of olive oil, and on the plate it gets a heavy grating of Parmesan, despite what the purists say about mixing cheese and seafood (if canned tuna can even be called that).

Two party-rental companies faxed price lists to me at work today, shedding more light on how things might quickly add up. There are security deposits, damage waivers, delivery fees. Do we need a thirty-by-thirty-foot tent, or thirty-by-fifteen? Do we want padded seats for $3.30 each, or do I let my ninety-eight-year-old grandmother sit on an unpadded seat for $2.50? Do we need center pole sleeves? Cathedral sides? Pole draping?

"What do the poles without draping look like?" Rich asks.

I have no idea. "I assume they look like . . . *poles.* Silver tent poles. Is anyone even going to notice them, when there are pretty set tables, flowers . . . ?" I ask, grabbing a pencil and scrap paper from the kitchen junk drawer to jot down what we need.

"Okay, food, alcohol, tent and rental stuff. Dress. Suit. Flowers. What else?" Rich says.

"Invitations, hotel, a rehearsal dinner—"

"I hate it when the rehearsal dinner is a mini version of the wedding. Can we just keep it to the people in the wedding, a normal dinner?" he says. That's fine with me. I want this to be easy, simple, fun.

After dinner I sit down at my desk, which I've pushed into my small walk-in closet, needing—as Virginia Woolf rightly pointed out long ago—a space of my own. Rich has taken to calling it my clubhouse, and, in a way, it is. I look again through Erin's list, and the prepared lists on wedding Web sites, and start a spreadsheet, guessing at the prices of things and including the items we forgot earlier. Music, photos, rings, a church donation, wedding-party gifts, a marriage license, haircuts, a manicure, some kind of car to get there in.

I print it and walk out to the living room, where Rich is sitting at his computer, getting ready to work.

"I think we can do it for ten thousand," I tell him. "I just need some kind of number to work with. Is that cool? Can we swing that?"

"Wow," Rich says, looking over the printout. "Um, sure. That's fine."

As I walk away, he puts his face in his hands and gives it a rough rub. Then he takes a deep breath and gets to work.

. . .

OUR MOTHER'S WEDDING gown was an object of great interest to my sisters and me. It had a slim, beaded bodice, long satin sleeves, and a fifteen-foot train. In 1966, her father paid a thousand dollars for it, which we understood was a generous sum for the time. Until I was nine years old, we lived in a gray house on a street called Sheppard Place, where the dress was stored in an unwieldy box on a high shelf in the linen closet, and occasionally Bridget would drag it down, or beg my mother to, so she could try it on. With the train draped over her arm, in just the way that showcased the beadwork, the two of them would dance a box step while Maria and our father and I looked on. Our mother would twirl Bridget and sing in her crooner's voice, "You're the end of the rainbow, my pot of gold. You're Daddy's little girl, to have and hold. . . ."

The night Bridget picked out her own gown, Maria and I had done something to infuriate our mother, so the four of us ate a quick dinner before they left for an appointment at a bridal shop, leaving Maria and me to clean up. Twenty minutes later, though, our mother's car crunched back up the gravel driveway and, working hard to swallow her anger, she announced, "This is an important moment for your sister. You two should be there."

The dress is sentimental to my mother, and she wants to pay for mine as her gift. For both these reasons, as well as to more fully escort her into the celebratory arena she was so slow to arrive at, I wish I'd found mine with her. But on the two Sundays that we visited New Jersey bridal shops together—one of them actually on the end of Sheppard Place, in what had been a bank whose parking lot we rode our bikes around in the evenings—neither of us saw anything we liked. Maria, recognizing this as her cue, booked a red-eye from Los Angeles.

At an ungodly hour, she buzzed the front door and I kissed her hello, complimented the soft leather traveling shoes she arrived in, and pointed her toward the prepared sofa bed, its duvet already folded back and waiting. Several hours of sleep, a slow breakfast, and, two showers later, we set off for midtown, I in the black boiled-wool jacket I long ago grew tired of, and she in an impossibly soft camel-colored wrap coat with a belted waist that actually has the effect of being slimming—a feat I'd never seen a non-celebrity accomplish with a winter coat. But such is the magic of Maria, who since settling in Los Angeles has developed a taste for luxuriousness that now makes her irritably intolerant of East Coast winters and the low-thread-count sheets in our mother's house. The upside to these discriminating standards, however, is that she now has an eye for finding just the right thing. While in recent years I've become almost incapable of bringing home anything to wear (Rich is sincerely baffled by how, no matter the determination I set off with, I come home empty-handed), to the point that Maria now barely cares to rifle through my closet when she arrives, and her little carry-on luggage contains more beautiful items (the very softest pajamas, the prettiest panties, the most non-itchy sweaters) than exist in my entire wardrobe. She has arrived to take me in hand, and I'm grateful.

We come up out of the subway on a stretch of Broadway in the garment district, link arms, and head for the Bridal Building, a twenty-four-story Hudsucker Industries–style tower of all things bridal: gowns, bridesmaids' dresses, limousine rentals, florists, photographers, videographers. Short of the groom, there's barely a bridal need it can't accommodate. Beyond the sweeping lobby, though, we find that it's simply a repurposed office building, with ugly industrial carpeting and a central elevator bay that the shops all circle around, one after another for floor after floor.

In the second shop we find our first possibility, a strapless, heavy satin gown constructed of two-inch bands, creating a look not unlike the Guggenheim. Two saleswomen with neat upsweeps gather around me at the three-sided mirror to make soft murmurs of approval, and in the fitting cubicle Maria and I agree to mentally bookmark it. On the hanger it's stunning, but once inside its intense scaffolding I feel like a girl playing dress-up. My mother wore a *gown,* Bridget wore a *gown,* and this tiered concoction, in which I maneuver like Scarlett O'Hara under a double layer of hoop skirts, is a *gown.* What I have in mind, I realize, is a dress.

We cover four floors in five hours and find nothing nicer than the Guggenheim dress, which each of us cools toward as we ascend the building. Hungry and tired, we agree to stop in one final shop before calling it day, and when we open the shop's door, it's comically bursting with gowns. They hang in long, dry-cleaner-like rows, pressed so tightly—their untamable skirts flaring outward—that they appear spring-loaded; a setup for Lucille Ball antics. Maria and I wade between the rows, giggling and strenuously pressing apart dresses to show each other particularly awful ones. Turning to leave, finally I notice a simple, pretty dress on a headless dress form near the register. When I look up to find Maria, she's examining a nearly identical one nearby. We like the top of one dress and the bottom of the other, both of which were designed by the diminutive, wrinkled seamstress sitting behind the clattering sewing machine in a side room.

"We can do! We can do!" the owner insists. It's *this* May, I tell her. "No problem, we can do! Eight hundred dollars, and you pick a veil for free."

When she hustles off to zip up a customer, Maria jokes in a whisper, "Maybe she'll bring down the price if you tell her Rich is Chinese!"

"Yes, we'll certainly be in the fold then. . . ." I whisper back in feigned agreement. But I can hear Rich forever complaining, "White people think all Asian people look the same," and feel compelled to add more seriously, "Actually, I think she's Korean."

My criteria for a dress have been that it be comfortable enough to dance in and low-key enough to not look silly in a backyard. Last night I went alone to a Vera Wang sample sale, where the dresses seemed to weigh twenty pounds each. Trying to keep them from sweeping the floor, I struggled to carry just two of them to the fitting room. The dresses made by the seamstress, though, are crushed silk and weigh nothing. There's no beading, no lace. The top of one is strapless, with loosely gathered folds (the fabric equivalent of combing fingers through hair), and the bottom of the other has a few soft darts and falls softly over a single crinoline, just skimming the floor. In other dresses I've felt pushed around, as if the dress were in charge; but in these I feel like me, only prettier.

Maria and I stare at my reflection under the communal fitting room's unforgiving light. "Maybe it's the folds, but doesn't this kind of remind you of the white dress the mean countess wears to the ball in *The Sound of Music*?"

Maria tilts her head. "That's a good thing, right?" We agree that I should buy the dress.

She unzips me, and while I pull on my jeans I toss the dress to her. "Let's see it on you now."

"Really?"

"It's so light—you have to feel it," I tell her, and she sets it on a chair and begins pulling off her boots.

It doesn't seem an odd thing to say until I catch the quick expression of another woman in the room, holding dresses for her daughter. Is the wedding dress so sacred as to preclude all normal shopping behavior? If we had been shopping for anything else, Maria would have tried on something similar, or we would have passed items back and forth over the fitting-room door. We're a year and six days apart, and we grew up with the same outfits, the same bedtimes, the same everything in different colors. Through the years of Pictionary popularity, we would be separated once Bridget complained, "They share a brain, it's not fair for them to be on the same team!" Until I left for college, we fought incessantly but were together constantly.

People still ask if we're twins, though feature for feature we don't actually look alike; we just speak the same way, laugh the same way, make the same expressions. While living on opposite coasts, even our handwriting merged to the point that our signatures (separately, we'd begun signing our first initial and last name) became identical. We noticed this a year ago, standing together at a shop counter signing credit-card slips. Pretending to be annoyed, she nudged me. "Stop trying to be me."

The big difference between us now is that she's four inches taller and definitely thinner, a true Angeleno. The last time we visited, Rich laughed from the kitchen, opening her refrigerator to find flaxseed, cranberry juice, wheat bread, and a watermelon. "I'm never home!" she defended herself, which is true. "I even stocked up before you came," she added, trying to keep a straight face. "The bread is for you guys."

Or maybe the big difference between us now is that I'm getting married and she's not. When my close friend Erin got married, Erin was as gracious about it as could be, but on the bus ride between New York and her home in Boston it finally sank in that there was a new person she called when something exciting or terrible or minorly ridiculous happened. For a decade, I was the one who knew the day-to-day minutiae of her life, but now it was someone else; it had been for a while, but it took Erin's wedding to finally put a spotlight on that fact for me.

I suppose I want Maria to try on the dress because it's fun to try on. And I want to see her in it, because seeing her is something like seeing me. And I want her to like it as much as I do, and to approve, maybe because I'm uneasy with the imbalance of our shopping mission. Marriage, I'm beginning to realize, is an exclusive thing—something I could see in her face as we ate breakfast in *our* place instead of *mine* (which in the past would have equaled nearly hers) and she remarked, watching me pull place mats from a drawer with folded table linens, "You've got quite a little household going here"—but I would hate for her to feel in any way excluded from my life.

Back at the apartment, Rich opens a bottle of wine to celebrate and, tired from our expedition, we decide to stay in and make dinner. Since she entered the apartment, Maria has been drawn to the dark-green kabocha squash in the big, shallow fruit bowl on the counter, inspecting, manhandling, and thumping it, and the three of us agree to have it sautéed with sage and farfalle, the bow-tie-shaped macaroni.

Maria is put on salad duty, and I fry three fresh sage leaves in a few tablespoons of olive oil, put the leaves on a paper towel to drain, and then sauté the cubed squash in the infused oil. Once it's soft, I add most of a can of rinsed white beans, a squeeze of lemon, the al dente farfalle, and a handful of roughly grated ricotta salada. When I plate it, I add a quick drizzle of olive oil, a turn of black pepper, and one of the sage leaves to each plate. Maria wrinkles her nose. "You people use too much oil."

This fruity, green olive oil is my new favorite discovery. It's from a Spanish grower who stamps the plot number on each bottle. "Do you know what I pay for this?" I ask her. "This is really good oil."

Rich smiles at his plate and announces, "I'm marrying the right sister."

Over dinner, they gang up to tease me about the wedding party, which is enormous—a thing I never thought I'd have. Like strawberry daiquiris and ribbons around ponytails, they're fine for other girls but not my style. And still . . .

"You'll have as many wedding-party members as guests!" Maria says, laughing, which is practically true. The saving grace is that I've thrown out the idea of bridesmaids' dresses, so there won't be an identical fleet beside me, just the individuals I love most. We're treating this wedding like a party—in the vein of a country wedding in Italy or France, where guests travel from the church to a home to eat, drink, dance, relax—so all formalities and traditions are getting a thorough once-over to determine their worth. Limousines and garters are definitely out, and an even number of bridesmaids and groomsmen isn't a priority (that they're one another's "dates" has always been weird to me). Considering the reason for the bridesmaids was actually what started the number climbing. If these are the closest witnesses to the oath I'm entering into, I thought, whom do I want standing beside me, sending out all their love and good energy? So now the list includes my two sisters; Rich's two sisters; my two nieces; Yasmine; Erin; my Los Angeles roommate, Christine; and Tonia, the most confident little spitfire of a woman I know, which makes me feel happy just thinking about her. Added to that are my brother-in-law, Wes; my nephew; a close friend of Rich's from Los Angeles; and two brothers he's been friends with since elementary school.

Further tarnishing my reputation, in keeping with the thought that these people will be exuding all their love and support, I have an idea that the wedding party should hold hands in a circle around us while we take our vows, which has Rich and Maria howling together at the corniness of it. I couldn't care less, though, and I laugh with them—I love this idea! I want all the good energy we can get.

It also thrills me to see Rich and Maria getting along so well. They're sometimes a little jokingly antagonistic toward each other, or I'll notice that Rich is a bit reserved with her in a way that he rarely is with anyone, except maybe my mother. When I asked him about this once, he said, "She's always watching me. It's not just hanging out, she's . . . she's judging."

"She's just looking out for me," I told him. "Everyone just wants to make sure you're being good to me."

"I know, but—*aren't I?* I totally like Maria, I really do. But your family, man . . ." He shook his head. "You all never let up. It's not just men who screw up relationships, you know."

After dinner, we change into pajamas, make up the sofa bed, and settle into it together for a movie, with me in the middle.

Maria and I like a dark room and wanted to turn off all the lights, but Rich insists that this is terrible for the eyes. "What about movie theaters!" we shot back with our identical logic, but he explained that that's a projector and this is a bulb, so it's like staring at a lightbulb in a dark room; so now we have a low lamp on. After we lie there for some time, I start to wonder if Rich has changed everything. Or if I've changed him, or he me? Or if maybe we can all just stay who we are, together.

...

Coming out of the subway after work, I head to the Depressed Grocer for a zucchini. I have a recipe for stuffing portobello caps with shredded zucchini, chopped tomatoes, onion, bread crumbs, eggs, and cheese. It was in an *LA Times* Food section six or seven years ago, with a grainy, unappetizing photo that made Rich laugh the first time he saw it. "How could you *possibly* have wanted to make this?" he asked, amazed. But it's good, and two caps with a salad make a filling meal; though he doesn't like to eat a lot of one flavor, so maybe I'll make a side of spaghetti with the rest of the tomatoes. Since this is just a half portion, they shouldn't bother his stomach.

I am the make-do eater between us, I often think, which reminds me of Natalia Ginzburg's wonderful back-and-forth essay, "He and I." "He likes tagliatelle, lamb, cherries, red wine. I like minestrone, bread soup, omelettes, green vegetables. He often says I don't understand anything about food, that I am like a great strong fat friar—one of those friars who devour soup made from greens in the darkness of their monasteries; but he, oh he is refined and has a sensitive palate."

It must be warmer than thirty-two degrees, because outside of her market fruit is piled in the green wooden trays. Wan, lumpy grapefruit for sixty-nine cents, lemons two for a dollar, ninety-nine cents a pound for Granny Smith apples waxed to such a shine they look as if they could bounce. Inside, the Depressed Grocer is behind the register, looking out the window but far off in thought. A cigarette is burning furiously in an ashtray on the counter, which I can't help loving a little. So often in this neighborhood we turn a corner and are confronted with a scene that makes us feel that we are living in a pocket of Eastern Europe. "Where else can you see that!" Rich will say, delighted by an eleven-by-seventeen-inch photograph of Pope John Paul, framed in gilded gold in a butcher-shop window. The uninspired architecture, the gray winter days, the snippets of Polish conversation we pass on the sidewalks. Even the hip twenty-somethings lend to the effect, with their penchant for dressing in layered early-MTV-era thrift clothes: polyesters, hip belts, cheap slouchy boots, Holly Hobbie skirts with abused leather purses.

When we first started coming to this neighborhood, for gallery openings Rich would hear about, it was fun to watch the style shift occur in the subway as the Upper West Side receded. The last Vuitton bag fell away with the switch to the L train, and after the ear-popping dip under the East River the doors would open at Bedford and every kid with a mohawk or a face tattoo, every girl pairing torn fishnets with white kid gloves and clogs, and all the skinny boys with black stretch jeans and legs thinner than my arms would file out. Each time, it was as though the one ultra-alternative, design-minded kid from every high school in America was now twenty-three and had agreed to ride the L train and exit at Bedford. The kids waiting on the station platform made it look like no other place in the city. Now, though, people who in 2000 I would have pegged for exiting at Bedford are staying on the train when the doors open, moving deeper into Brooklyn, and a growing percentage of the crowd exiting the train in the evenings looks as bland as I do, coming from the office in kitten heels, jeans, and an Ann Taylor blouse.

I put the zucchini on the counter, and she comes out of her thought and turns to me. "How are you?" I ask, digging through my bag for my wallet. She frowns deeply into her creases. She's probably only in her forties, but there's an exhaustion in her face that makes me think she has seen a lifetime of terrible things.

"They take half of my money and give it to my sister in Israel!" she blurts, and then pouts. I have no idea how to respond to this.

"Oh. Um. That doesn't sound fair." I pause, floundering. "I'm sure she must appreciate it, though. It's really generous of you. . . ."

"Yes, *but* . . ." she says, handing me my change and then dropping her bottom heavily onto her wooden stool, "I am person, *too*. I need money, *too*."

"Of course!" I say, in full agreement. "Of course . . ." Which feels inadequate but seems to appease her. Then, after a few silent beats, "Well, have a good night."

"Yes, and you," she responds, the proprietress again, and gives me her slow forward nod.

. . .

WILLIAMSBURG IS ONE of a handful of neighborhoods that are about as close as you can get to the city without being in the city. Which, while not its single recommendable asset, is certainly its most striking. Manhattan is a constant presence across the river. Aside from the occasional fleet of sirens on the FDR Drive, crawling up the city's eastern edge, the island's incredible noise is swallowed by the distance and the water, so most days it stands in all its physical glory, wondrously silent.

On clear afternoons it can appear sweet and contained, a Lego construction or an architect's model, complete with small moving parts and a cotton wisp over the Con Edison smokestacks. But against a black night sky it's the sprawling, moneyed stuff of postcards, lit and pulsing from bottom to top, with its four East Side bridges lying on the river like extravagant jewelry. Though the next night, behind a gray drizzle, with only the glowing top of the Empire State Building piercing the haze between us, it can seem an ominous Gotham, calling for a superhero's rescue.

"Isn't it funny that this is the apartment we'll tell our kids we lived in when we first got married?" Rich sometimes says. When his parents first married, they rented a redwood house in Blacksburg, Virginia, that his mother painted light pink. "I thought it was very American," she once told me, laughing at herself. She arrived from China through San Francisco and wanted a pretty pastel house like the ones she'd seen there. "I didn't know you're only supposed to *stain* redwood!" My parents bought a house in the Italian neighborhood of Bay Ridge, Brooklyn, with a basement apartment they rented to a young lawyer who later became a fairly well-known judge. But then a nearby building was torn down, the mice relocated, the lawyer moved out, and my parents sold the house and moved to New Jersey.

What will we tell our kids? That on summer nights we'd carry a bottle of wine to the roof-deck and be amazed to find it empty? That we'd pull folding chairs to where the view was best and take in the full sweep of Manhattan from the Williamsburg Bridge to the Queensboro, toasting our luck and imagining holding the wedding up there? (A special table for the neighbors. Good Polish beer and pierogi. Tattoos instead of rings.) There are rumors that the waterfront is going to be developed; by the time we tell this story, will it be unimaginable that there was ever a view from this old building?

The neighborhood's older Polish residents still live and work among the influxes of young people, which makes it feel like nowhere else I've ever lived. These twenty-somethings—so thin, so tragically hip!—increase exponentially come the weekend, leaving not a café seat to be had by a person with a laptop trying to escape her windowless living room for an hour. Some neighbors begrudged the changes of the past few years, which we're a part of, and nowhere do I feel the resentment more strongly than in the bakery, where the women behind the counter—women my age and younger, with hard Polish accents and an impenetrable aloofness—are curt with me, bored, look elsewhere when I point in the dessert case at which of the long loaf pans of cakes I'd like a few inches of.

But I can barely imagine the joy the grown children of the factory owners must have felt, as the albatrosses they inherited turned to real-estate gold. It's common to hear people refer to buildings by what was once made in them. "We live in the girdle factory," say a pretty couple we meet through a neighbor. Others live in the pencil factory, the chocolate factory, the old mill building. Gretsch guitars were famously

made in one building, and OLD DUTCH MUSTARD CO, in flaking
white paint, tall as a man, is still at the top of another await-
ing development. Online, we discover that the gutted building's selling price is twenty-five million dollars. Which sags
the jaw, but then makes better sense once we guess how
many apartments it will hold.

There has barely been a time when these few miles, and
the people in them, weren't being exploited. As far back as
1638, a wily General Kieft from the Dutch West India Company bought this portion of the Brooklyn waterfront from a
group of Native Americans from the Canarsee tribe for
"eight fathoms of duffels, eight strings of wampum, twelve
kettles, eight chip-axes and eight hatchets and some knives,
beads and awls," I find in some historical records at the library. The trade took place on the New Jersey coast near
present-day Hoboken, which Kieft also thought rather nice
and tried to make available by later sending back a group to
slaughter everyone living there. At first a neighboring tribe
was suspected, but once word got out that the white men
were to blame, the retribution of river tribes did much to
slow the development of Kieft's new Brooklyn property,
which he named Boswijck.

After the British conquered the Dutch's holdings, the
name was Anglicized to Bushwick Shore, and for the next
140 years it was mostly used as farmland, which was convenient; farmers rowed down and across the river and sold
their goods in lower Manhattan. As development in Manhattan crept northward, a wealthy developer noted Bushwick
Shore's potentially lucrative location and purchased thirteen
acres, which he renamed Williamsburgh after his friend
Jonathan Williams, an engineer and the grand-nephew of

Benjamin Franklin, who agreed to perform the survey. The area was incorporated as the Village of Williamsburgh within the Town of Bushwick in 1827, and its population began to grow.

The afternoon that Rich and I became Brooklyn residents, the moving truck driver jutted his chin toward the railing as we crossed the Queensboro Bridge. "You see that?" he said to the two of us, sandwiched beside him in the truck's cab. "It flows both ways."

Shimmering in full sun, the fast-moving river looked cleaner than each of us knew it to be, and for the first time I noticed the crooked seam up its center and each side moving its own way. Which seemed an exotic thing for New York. Friends once returned from a trip to the Amazon with photos of a river that also flowed both ways and glowed with phosphorescence—or was it the fish that glowed?—and over a dinner we'd marveled at the stunning seam where the water divided itself up.

It was this river that determined the fate of the Brooklyn waterfront. Carved by glaciers, its bays are incredibly deep, which, combined with its proximity to Manhattan and the direct route it offered to the Erie Canal, made it ideal for industry. In the first half of the nineteenth century, five "black arts," as a poet once called them, set down roots on the Williamsburg waterfront: cast iron, porcelain, publishing, petroleum refining, and glass. A table service Mary Todd Lincoln ordered for the White House came from an area glassmaker.

In 1840, Williamsburg became its own town, and by 1850 it was number twenty-three on the U.S. Census of one hundred largest cities. By 1855, it had grown to the point of needing a proper city government and so was folded into Brooklyn, which by 1860 had climbed to number three on the census. The waterfront was thriving, and wealthy industrialists and professionals embraced it. Pfizer Pharmaceuticals, Corning Glass Works, Domino Sugar, and the Schlitz Brewery were all founded near Williamsburg's Broadway. Charles Pratt established Astral Oil Works (later Standard Oil, then ExxonMobil), and Cornelius Vanderbilt and the railroad magnate James Fisk built mansions on the waterfront.

In 1903, the Williamsburg Bridge was completed (though shoddily, necessitating an overhaul for its one-hundredth birthday) and connected Williamsburg's Broadway to Manhattan's Lower East Side. Suddenly the poor immigrants and second-generation Americans who had been crowded to the edges of eastern Manhattan had a steel footpath out. In little time the poor moved over, the wealthy fled, and Williamsburg (which somewhere along the way lost its *h*) became one of the most densely populated neighborhoods in the United States. And that was before the refugees of World War II began streaming over in search of relatives.

I imagine this was when our older Polish neighbors arrived. While the converted factory buildings are almost exclusively filled with young people, the neighborhood's lines of skinny row houses are mostly home to generations of Polish families. Even the teenagers and children, surely born here, speak Polish on the street. If we had moved ten blocks east, though, our neighbors would be Italians; ten south, Dominicans and Puerto Ricans; and, south of them, Hasidic Jews. Similarly, when my father arrived in Brooklyn from Italy in the mid-1940s, the neighborhood his parents chose was so thoroughly Italian that my grandmother never learned to speak English.

"Your mother and I thought we were the successes, getting out of Brooklyn," my father has told me, laughing and awed by the current real estate market's take on the Carroll Gardens brownstone he grew up in. A cousin had once encouraged my grandfather to buy. "'Fifteen thousand dollars, for *these* dumps!'" he tells me, repeating his father's words. "Now they're worth three million." I suspect it's closer to four, but say nothing. Still, he can't imagine coming back, and I can't imagine ever leaving.

When I first arrived in Manhattan in 2000, during the thickest heat of August, I woke up early each morning with my stomach still churning over the decision I'd made. It became a ritual to pull on a skirt and flip-flops and be downstairs while the sidewalk was still wet, rinsed by the night doorman before he signed off his shift, and the air still had a hint of coolness to it. I'd walk to my bodega (the closest bodega) and buy a fresh baguette or three square ciabatta rolls for a dollar, which would last me through lunch and dinner; passing up a weekly bag of sandwich bread for this daily ritual gave me a ridiculous amount of pleasure. Afterward, I'd join the line of construction workers and morning doormen in the slip of storefront under my building, and we'd stand together watching bacon and eggs sputter on the searing black cooktop that kept the Chinese cashier and her old mother fanning themselves. The two young Mexican chefs would know, with a nod to me and without my saying so, that I wanted an egg and American cheese on a fresh kaiser roll, which came with a decent enough cup of coffee for $1.99—a deal that billowed my heart with optimism for this city.

When my sisters and I were girls, our father would take us on a Sunday-morning walk for Italian bread from the bakery, and then a newspaper for himself and a candy for each of us at a shop that smelled of newsprint and the cigars that were sold in the back. Walking alone down Amsterdam Avenue those mornings, with fresh bread under my arm and a coffee in my hand, it would startle me to feel so much my father's daughter. We are both early risers and delighters in routines, and I'd feel distinctly aware that I was shadowing his steps as a younger man.

Likewise, during my second semester at Columbia, I won a fellowship that involved doing research for an editor at *The New York Times,* and on my biweekly trips to his office I'd sometimes imagine my mother—not yet engaged, young and lovely under her tall, coiffed beehive—hurrying down Forty-second Street toward her old job in the McGraw-Hill Building. It was the single way that, however briefly, our experiences ran parallel, and I liked having this in common with her. I was young, and I was proud of being in graduate school; my parents have a high school education, and, in succeeding a step beyond their successes, I was fulfilling the role of the next generation.

When I left Los Angeles, I imagined I was leaving the comfort of my mother and sisters for a city of strangers; but in New York people looked and dressed and spoke like my relatives and parents, and nowhere else has ever more instantly felt like home. Though somedays it feels still more awkward to be so intentionally creating a different life for myself—so conscious of not traveling down the paths my parents carved—in the one place where I feel their presence everywhere.

It has taken me years to realize it, maybe because I never actually see either of them here, but so much of what appeals to me about New York is rooted in my love for them.

. . .

TODAY IS ONE of those unexpected warm days that show up while gray snow is still piled in the corners and send everyone hurrying outside, optimistically coatless, to sit at quickly dragged-out café tables before the temperature falls with the sun and we'll likely see fresh snow in the morning. But I'll take it. I lower the bedroom windows halfway, to air out the apartment, and then make cold soba noodles with soy-honey dressing from the Sybil Kapoor cookbook *Taste*. The soba are a throwback to the summer and our first weeks living to-gether. We moved to Williamsburg for the apartment, which was larger than everything we saw in Manhattan, but it was through those first muggy weeks, playing tennis after work (me terribly, Rich well) with a shuffled deck of skinny twenty-somethings in short-shorts, deeply tanned older Pol-ish men, slim housewives in tennis whites, and the full view of the Empire State Building standing directly across the river, that we fully fell for the neighborhood.

Before heading out the door, I'd cover diced scallions and cubed tofu with a cooled sauce of honey, ginger, soy sauce, sesame oil, lemon juice, and red-pepper flakes, toss it all with some flash-cooled and drained soba noodles in my largest pasta bowl, and leave it to marinate until we returned, hot and happy, when it was finally too dark to see the ball.

Walking home, we'd pass Hasidic teenagers playing half-court basketball, with both teams in a uniform of black pants, white dress shirts, black yarmulkes, and long face-framing curls. Across the street, the park lights would be up over a baseball game, and after each crack of the bat would come whistles and applause from supporters in the crab-grassy sidelines. Across the street from them, on a badly maintained soccer field, Latino players might be scrimmaging a Japanese team while a tall group of Poles looked on; joggers on the red rubber track patiently swerved around bicyclists on training wheels; and girls with tight ponytails leaned on their handlebars watching men in baggy jeans play competitive games of handball. On two far benches, a cluster of elderly Italians, their waistbands high on their stomachs, would be enjoying the twilight, their bocce balls still showing the final frame in the sand.

Just before our front door, the day having finally gone dark, we would find Emily, our elderly neighbor, sitting on the bench in her few feet of front yard and waiting to say hello. On our nearly treeless street, she turned her concrete stoop into an overrun Eden of potted pink and red blossoms, sunflowers, herbs, and purple morning glories, to the point that her front door became inaccessible and she relied solely on a basement entrance. Despite her English extending to little beyond salutations and responses to compliments on her garden, she's enthusiastic for conversation. "Hello, Richie!" she'd call out when she spotted us, her cloud of white hair making her more visible in the dark.

We'd shower and dress and, while the air conditioner hummed away and order was again restored, I'd toast a square of nori over a stove burner and with kitchen shears snip it into shimmering black-green strips over our respective piles of soba. With a cold Corona with lime, it was the perfect dinner, and we ate it constantly through the last hot weeks of summer, which had built into them a clear sense of being the happy beginning of something that would not always be so simple.

Tonight I top the soba noodles with slices of sweetened omelet-style egg—my loose interpretation of tamago— which adds protein but potentially screws up Kapoor's very intentional recipe, which is all about juxtaposing very basic tastes so that together they become something more wonderful. A nice idea.

With each new place my mother has lived, she hops between churches until she finds one she likes. "I need to feel spiritually fed," she insists. The older I get, I find I also need to feel fed—indeed, fortified—by the place where I live. In the news after September 11, there were reports of South Asians in various suburbs being singled out and harassed. Taking a walk to clear our heads during those days, Yasmine told me, "New York is the one city where I never feel I stick out. Here, everyone blends in." Maybe Rich and I take for granted that we're living in a time and a place where marrying a person of a different race couldn't possibly feel like less of a big deal. Or maybe taking it for granted is the perfect goal. When we first started dating, a friend giggled to me over the phone about Rich's last name, which is the Chinese equivalent of Jones, or Smith; she wasn't at all being mean, the name just felt entirely foreign to her. In the way that some people say nothing is taboo anymore, there's little left in New York that feels *other*. Which is a comfort I didn't know to expect. My mother laments the money that she imagines we're "throwing away" on rent. "For that price, you could have a beautiful four-bedroom house out here!" she tells me. Even beyond the Richard Yates–style anxiety this fills me with, I wouldn't know what to do with a lawn or the suburbs or all those bedrooms. Right now, the life we're figuring out together fits best here, where we are both as odd and as unremarkable as the next couple.

...

AFTER A WEEKLONG bout of the flu, Valentine's Day is upon us. We're in saving mode, so no gifts, we agreed, except dinner. Though I give Rich DVDs of a transplanted British television show and, returning from work, I find that he has bought me a cupcake for a snack and a chocolate cake for after dinner. Following our friend Matsu's recommendation, we have a reservation at a Japanese restaurant in the meat-packing district, which—the gray afternoon having given way to a stormy night—suddenly feels very far away.

As we come out of the subway together, the wind is whipping and flips the umbrella inside out twice before the restaurant's door, though even when it's right-side up we barely manage to stay dry. Once in the foyer, though, the mood is Zen, with complementing textures and low lighting. The walls and the floor around the bar are a beautiful dark bamboo, and in the ladies' room, drying off, I'm mesmerized by a troughlike sink tiled in bright teal. We order a Daiginjo sake and split appetizers of monkfish liver (which is rich but cut perfectly with vinegar and wasabi); oysters on the half shell roasted with miso; and eel baked in puff pastry, all fantastic. Then Rich has a filet mignon and I inhale a fillet of black cod soaked in miso, which is so delicious I wish I could order two more.

The dining room is ringed with romantically lit booths filled with good-looking couples. This is the first Valentine's Day in years that I haven't secretly wondered if Rich was going to pop the question, if a large box actually held something small. The question has been asked and answered, the ring's on my finger, and we are a secure couple, eating. Rich has graciously given me the "good" seat—the one facing out toward the restaurant—and I have a perfect view of how young and confident the women all around us look, their faces bright with expectation. As conflicted as I've felt about getting married, even I eventually began to feel the stress of not having a ring. And still, sitting here I feel a sudden flash of jealousy for what seems to me their youth and wide-open options. I finally crossed over, and now I have the audacity to look back. Is the engagement the pinnacle *and* the dénouement? Is it all a slow roll downhill from here?

Rich smiles at me. "What are you thinking?"

"This place is nice," I say, and he nods in agreement. At least he got my best year. Twenty-three. How pretty I was at twenty-three! So young and fresh, and so fit. I swam a lot that year, and ran on packed sand at the beach. Even my terrible thighs were lean and tan at twenty-three. And now what? There are mornings when I look in the mirror and can't believe these puffy eyes are mine. In fifth grade I gave drawing a try, and one Sunday afternoon I sketched my mother during a rare nap. Later, admiring my efforts, she asked gently, "Why did you draw me with two sets of eyes?" All confidence, I explained, "Oh, those aren't eyes, those are the *bags* under your eyes."

Poor Rich, he's stuck with me. Or maybe he'll get rid of me? I peaked five years ago, but he's becoming more handsome with age. I can see it in people's faces when they meet us—he's become the better-looking between us now. Is it true that all men, even happy men, cheat? There's that perfect line in *Anna Karenina* when Levin and Oblonsky are finishing their enormous lunch and Levin likens cheating on a woman he loves to stealing a roll on his way home, full as he is. To which Oblonsky, eyes twinkling, replies, "Ah, but rolls sometimes smell so that one can't resist them!"

Maybe this wry mood is the conclusion to having been sick all week while Rich has been incredibly busy. Twice in three days he drove four hours to test-drive a car, then four hours home, and then spent the night writing up the article. Inheriting my flu would have derailed his packed schedule, so he gave me a wide berth. Which, while understandable, felt crummy when I was sick and even worse when I was sick and achy with "girl problems." Tonight, I'm also feeling fat from a week of no gym, owing to being sick, plus bloated as a hot-water bottle, plus dowdy in old clothes and stressed about wedding money. I've discovered that caterers cost more than I'd budgeted for.

"You should finish this," I say, nudging the sake bottle toward Rich. "Sake with sinus medicine probably wasn't the best idea."

But then we go home and watch the new DVD in bed on a laptop while eating my gifted chocolate cake, and together they're the best part of my week and the perfect end to a night with the wind howling against the windows.

WALNUT TARTS

WHEN MY FATHER'S mother turned ninety-nine, she said that she wanted new shoes for her birthday. He brought her shopping, and she picked out navy pumps to match her purse. "You're ninety-nine!" he'd barked. "You can't wear heels!" They went home with flat shoes, and the following week she made my aunt exchange them for pumps. The style of an Italian woman is not a thing to be trifled with.

Given that she spoke almost no English, I imagine my sisters and I would hardly have felt as close to our grandmother had she not been an extraordinarily good cook. There are too many wonderful dishes that no one can reproduce exactly. Her fried zucchini puffs were bouncy as sponge cake the next day, and her ravioli— thin, pale squares, with perfect zigzag edges from the tool she cut the dough with—dissolved on the tongue.

Each December she prepared maybe ten types of cookies, dozens and dozens of them, all of which froze well and enabled her to set out a mixed plate for anyone who walked through the door. A glazed almond cookie, small as a lug nut, rated high, but my absolute favorite was her walnut tarts.

When my sister Bridget called me one December to say that our grandmother had passed away, two months shy of her one hundredth birthday, I was in my kitchen with a friend, baking her walnut tarts.

CRUST:

> 8 ounces cream cheese
> 1 stick butter
> 1 cup flour

FILLING:

> 1 egg, beaten
> ¾ cup brown sugar
> ½ cup chopped pecans or walnuts, or a
>   combination of the two
> 1 teaspoon vanilla extract
> 1 teaspoon butter, melted

PREHEAT THE OVEN TO 350 DEGREES. For this recipe you'll need a mini muffin tin (two, ideally). Put these in the refrigerator. Then blend the crust ingredients until smooth. If, like me, you tend to have warm hands, wash them under cold water. Drop teaspoonfuls of dough into each muffin cup and press the dough with your fingertips until each one is like a mini piecrust. Don't press them so thin that you can see the gray of the muffin tin; the thickness of a navel orange peel is about right.

Put the muffin tins back into the refrigerator while you make the filling, simply mixing the ingredients together. Spoon the filling into each little pie shell, leaving a little space before the top of the crust. Bake for 20 to 30 minutes, until the crust is light brown.

These will not taste like my grandmother's. Whether she was the type of person to intentionally leave out an ingredient or she just had a touch that none of us can match, I can't say. They're still good, though, they freeze well, and in a cookie tin or a glass jam jar they make a gift that anyone who likes nuts should be thrilled to receive.

. . .

ON A WEDNESDAY NIGHT, MY MOTHER CALLS. "HI, BABE, what are you doing?" she asks. We're standing at the kitchen counter eating blue cheese, a Bosc pear, walnuts, and Wasa bread off the cutting board.

"Figuring out what to have for dinner," I tell her. I spent forty dollars at Pitts last night, but apparently managed only to equip us with breakfast, lunch, and cocktail-party fare. My two ideas for more substantial meals were rejected earlier (the first as too fussy, the second too heavy), so now we're snacking as a delay tactic. "We're still fine-tuning the dinner situation."

She laughs an unexpectedly girlish laugh, enjoying this glimpse behind our closed door. That I'm a woman with a home and a man in it is still a novelty to her, but finally this is something about my life she can relate to. "Well, I used to make a list on Sunday of all the meals I wanted to make for the week, and then shopped for it all at once," she offers. "Why don't you do that?"

I try to imagine Rich, who dreads discussing dinner before his stomach begins to growl, having discussed tonight's dinner last Sunday. Though, to be fair, I also find it stifling to have my meals planned so rigidly; it's bad enough that the rest of my days are. Plus, the city encourages a spontaneity that it feels a waste (on the order of not smelling roses) to ignore. There are fruit and vegetable carts on random corners, weekly farmers' markets to bump into, and small grocers and mom-and-pop bodegas with their produce abutting sidewalk traffic. How much more appetizing it is to see the season's first artichokes, or baby zucchini, or a pretty ruffle of chard, and then bring it home to cook that night while it's at its freshest and I still have an excited taste for it. (The same chard two nights later can become a nagging guilt, insisting I would have done better to throw the money away—or to spend it on lottery tickets, as one friend suggested—than miss the short window that organic allows and let it wilt in the vegetable drawer.)

And for last-minute convenience there's no better friend than the bodega, which for me is a distinctly New York experience. I loved my old bodega near 9J. It carried an excellent rice pudding, with fresh grated nutmeg on top, and had a ginger-colored cat that liked to sleep on the pile of *The New York Times* by the door. It was roughly the size of a suburban master-bedroom suite, but it managed to squeeze inside nearly everything a person living in two hundred square feet could go looking for. The luxury of selection was rare, but whether it was cake frosting, a toilet brush, saffron, or index cards, strategically stacked toward the ceiling or cantilevered over the register, it was there.

Leaving that bodega each day with a ten-dollar bag of groceries, I often thought of my mother overloading a grocery cart each week and stuffing the car trunk to capacity, feeding five of us for a hundred dollars a week. In suburban

New Jersey, a daily trip to the market wouldn't have made sense, but here the reverse is true.

"I've thought about it," I tell her. I don't say that dinner in our home also isn't nearly as straightforward as it was in hers. My four grandparents were from neighboring fishing villages in Italy, so my parents grew up eating similar things; when they married, the dishes my mother knew how to cook were almost exactly the ones my father had always eaten. Their tastes and expectations at the table were one of the few ways in which they were actually alike.

My meat-free diet is also an increasing cause for our stale-mates. I stopped eating red meat when I was fifteen, as a boycott against an industry I'd read was devastating the environment. Fast-food chains were razing expanses of rain forest (which, with its shallow root system, never recovers) for cattle grazing. Then there was the waste and the carbon dioxide to account for, and the difficulty of knowing the conditions the animals had been subjected to—which, whatever they were, were condoned with each purchase. After learning that chickens' beaks were clipped off, so they didn't damage each other's flesh when packed tightly into pens, I gave up poultry as well. *Free-range, local, organic,* and *sustainably raised* have since come into my vocabulary and address my concerns, but after fourteen years without it I'm not quite ready for the transition back to meat. Seafood, of course, has its own slew of issues (overfishing, pollutants, the stunning waste created by farmed fish, which exceeds that of human cities), but keeping my protests to only two major dinner categories originally made things less trying for my mother, as it does for us now. Though Rich will still sometimes say, peering into the refrigerator at our dinner options, "Dinner would be so much easier if you ate meat. Other people don't have this problem because they just make some kind of meat protein, throw a starch and a vegetable on the plate, and they're done. Without meat, everything's so much more *time-consuming*."

Beyond the meat issue (or maybe partly because of it), there is also the newly emerged reality of how exhausting it is to work all day, commute home, change, go to the gym, shower, dress again, and then cook a decent meal, *every day*. And, added to this, is the dish-washing issue. A recent conversation:

> ME: How about romaine-wrapped cod fillets for din-
> ner? The fish steams inside the romaine, which
> draws out the sweetness of the lettuce.
> HIM: *(Pulling back the corners of his mouth in an "I-don't-
> know-about-this" way.)* That sounds like a lot of
> work. Like a lot of *dishes*.
> ME: So I'm supposed to think in advance about din-
> ner, not spend too much, find something we'll
> both eat, have it be filling enough for you, quick
> enough for me to make after work, *and* make it
> using as few dishes as possible.
> HIM: Yes!
> ME: *(Menacing glare.)*
> HIM: You're just making things that are too complex!
> *(Encouraging smile.)* Just keep it simple.
> ME: *(More menacing glare.)*

I hang up with my mother, and it's T-minus-thirteen minutes until our guilty Wednesday-night pleasure of *The O.C.* I make

a side dish of spaghetti squash with parsley-walnut pesto—
the one thing in *The Gourmet Cookbook* that we seem to have
all the ingredients for—and grilled-cheese sandwiches with
provolone and quartered dill pickles. Both of which actually
turn out quite well.

"Oh, very nice!" Rich says, admiring my handiwork as he
hurries our two dishes to the coffee table, which he's set with
place mats, napkins, and water glasses. A low flame, a lid,
cooking spray, and more than my normal patience are the secrets to my grilled-cheese success.

Later, Rich is on the phone with his parents (they pick up
on two landlines and the three of them talk at once). They're
all speaking Mandarin, but I can follow the conversation
through the words he can't translate. *Grilled cheese. Spaghetti
squash. Pesto.* I can tell by the tone of his voice that he's insisting both were good. Eventually, the conversation moves on
to Manny Ramirez, and I go back to my closet to write in my
journal.

Getting ready for bed later, I ask him, mostly joking, "So,
do you tell them what we have for dinner on nights that I
manage to feed you well? What did they say?"

He looks up from his laptop, adjusting his expression to
an overly charming smile. "My mom just said, '*Oh . . .* ' " he
says with a little laugh. It's the kind of polite, drawn-out *Oh* a
person uses when in no way relating to the thing she's been
told. We exchange a long look, and I'm not sure whether to
feel more embarrassed or annoyed.

"Did you tell them I had two other perfectly good ideas
but the son they raised is a fussy little brat?"

He gets up grinning and gives me a hug, but I let my arms
stay slack, which he solves by tossing them up around himself

and finally making me laugh. "My funny little baby . . ." he says. "Don't be so defensive. Nobody's judging you."

Thirty minutes later, we're lying in bed reading when the phone rings again. Rich does some uh-huhing and speaks a few curt lines of Mandarin. "Babah, I know!" he says finally, before hanging up with, "Okay, okay . . . good night."

"What was that?"

He gets back into bed, rearranging the pillows behind his head. "They wanted to make sure I understand the importance of getting enough iron in my diet," he says, splitting the pages of his book and returning to it with a sigh. Maybe a little advanced planning isn't the worst idea.

. . .

MY FATHER CALLS me at work. "What are you doing?" he asks.

"I'm working," I tell him.

"You women in my life are always working!" This is his big joke. A few years ago, he retired from the New York utility where he'd spent thirty-eight years and moved to Florida with his new wife. She's the CEO of a health-care organization that demands endless compassion, intelligence, and patience, traits that, I suspect, assist her in her personal life as well. He likes to say, "I tell her, 'Kathryn! You're the boss! Who's going to say anything if you don't do the work?' "

My father emigrated through Ellis Island at the age of seven, not speaking a word of English, and started working immediately, shining shoes and bagging groceries after school. He was hired at the utility company straight out of the army, drove a cab at night for extra money when my mother first became pregnant, worked overtime during snowstorms, took side jobs when they came his way. Some people have a hard time adjusting to retirement, but it fits him like a robe he's been waiting his entire life to relax into. Kathryn leaves him each morning to his coffee and his news-paper, maybe a little dusting and some laundry, and on Wednesdays his volunteer docent job at the local aquarium, where when he doesn't know the answer to a child's question he makes something up. After the newspaper there's a brisk two-mile walk, a few laps in the pool, a shower and a shave, and then, standing in his living room looking out toward the lanai, he dispatches his daily social calls.

"Working . . ." he repeats. Then, meaning to sound friendly, he barks, "So, are you two okay? Are you eating meat now? What are you eating?"

My mind goes blank. What are we eating?

"Yes, we're fine, we're eating. He has a hamburger for lunch, or some prosciutto on salad. There's plenty to eat in this world besides meat, you know."

But he's not satisfied. Or maybe he's genuinely confused. "So, for instance, what did you have for dinner last night?"

We seem to have lost the thread this week. On the heels of the grilled cheese, last night we both worked late, the dinner conversation didn't happen until the night was too far along, and then none of my suggestions sounded filling to Rich, so in the end we went our separate ways. (This is something we literally say: "Let's go our separate ways.") I reverted to my old reliable and poached two eggs, which I ate over a salad of frisée and mesclun with the last piece of bread in the house, and he made himself a skirt steak that he'd bought that after-noon, which he ate with the extra salad I'd tossed. We'd sat down together, though, and there was some open red wine and the votives were lit, so it had seemed we were still a decent household. But this hardly exemplifies my point, so I lie.

"*Pasta e fagioli* with popovers and a salad," I say. This is a classic winter dinner in my mother's repertoire.

"*Oh,*" he says brightly, clearly assuaged. "Oh, very good." Then, moving on from that, "You know, I make this very nice side dish now . . . *roasted asparagus.* I never really liked them before, but this way they're delicious. I saw it on that Mario show. Do you know he's from Puglia?"

Life, bizarrely, has delivered us to this similar place at a similar time. This is my father, who, during his twenty-three years of marriage to my mother, likely made no more than four hot meals for himself or anyone else. But now I'm on his list, and he calls once a week to talk about what each of us is making for dinner. I realize that neither of us liked asparagus because we were used to my mother's, which were gray-green and limp, probably because her mother prepared them that way, because the Pugliese like their vegetables well done. (Surely Mario Batali, who is actually several generations removed from Puglia—if that's where his family is really even from—is an exception.) It wasn't until I was seventeen and had asparagus at a friend's house, served bright green and crisp, that I also discovered they were actually delicious.

"I like to simmer them in a few tablespoons of water for just a minute," I tell him. "Then I put them in an ice bath, dry them, and drizzle them with olive oil, salt, and ground pepper. On a hot night, with a few little boiled potatoes and some smoked salmon on dark bread—or Wasa, do you know that kind of wide cracker?—with a little sour cream and dill, they make a nice dinner."

"Huh," he says. He's a better listener on the phone than I ever remember him being. "I'll have to try that."

Coming up out of the subway after work, my father's words are still with me, and I stop at the first of two Polish butcher shops on Bedford, the neighborhood's main street, preferring this one simply for its entertaining odds and ends for the homesick expatriate, including Polish-language equivalents of *Hello!* and *OK!* I ask the butcher's wife for something that I can add to a vegetable soup, and she turns to the rods in her window display, where the sausages hang in twos, like acrobats straddling a trapeze bar. They deepen in color from left to right, ranging from a gaunt beige to a rich mottled burgundy, and she chooses a smooth pink pair for me.

"*Huneee*," she says, separating my one from its twin with a quick snap like a party balloon. "What are you going to do with only one *sauseege*?"

I scan my brain for the answer she's looking for. Does she mean how am I going to prepare it, or why don't I want more? "I can't really eat more than that," I tell her, my second lie of the day. It seems simpler than explaining that I'm just adding it to Rich's portion of the soup so it's more filling for him; and that I believe meat should be more of a side dish than an entrée; and that who even knows what's inside that little log she's so tenderly folding into crisp white butcher paper. She smiles at me weakly.

Between us is an enormous, cold meat case filled with items I could spend an afternoon examining. A loosely wrapped headcheese is composed of so many colors and gelatinous textures that it brings to mind the Italian nougat candies that circulate at Christmas—white as spackling, with bright-colored gumdrops suspended in its firmament. I flash to an image of myself as this woman's loyal apprentice, the two of us in white aprons, months spent learning to expertly sharpen flashing knives against each other, and this mysterious, refrigerated world whose secrets she would introduce me to, revealing the kinder face of meat.

But, "Next!" I'm gathering the nerve to ask her what she would do with the kielbasa when her gruff husband, frowning, hurries the line along. (Did I just order the equivalent of half a loaf of bread?) The man behind me steps up to place a loud order in Polish, and I quickly pay, thank her, and get out.

After the gym, I put together a simple vegetable soup (onion, carrot, celery, zucchini, white beans, bay leaf), and while it simmers I unwrap the kielbasa, which is fresher than I could have imagined. It's delicate and fragrant, and as I slice it on a diagonal I can see peppercorns and whole fennel seeds. "Soft as a baby's bottom" goes through my mind several times, and I bring my face down to the board to inhale. In a large skillet, I brown the kielbasa, remove the slices, wipe out some of its little grease, pour in half the soup, and, when it's back to a simmer, lower back in the kielbasa slices.

Rich sets the table, and I serve up our respective bowls with grated Parmesan, cracked pepper, and a drizzle of olive oil over mine. I've tossed a salad and toasted four slices of the Polish bakery's country-rye bread, which I always fear will be as abrasive and unappealing as packaged rye but is consistently softer and more subtle, something closer to sourdough. It's a distinctly peasant meal, which I like. The Italians and the Chinese both have traditions of a peasant cuisine—or *la cucina povera,* as the Italians call it—that speaks to a culinary industriousness and a people who know how to do much with little. Secretly, it pleases me to think this strain runs through us both.

And still, I'm surprised by the delight with which Rich surveys the meal and then smiles at me. "Oh, *very* nice . . ." he says, in the drawn-out way that makes the words feel like a pat on the back; it's a nice intonation that his parents also use. *We are back on track, smooth sailing.*

We sit, I say grace for us both, and we clink glasses. "To the chef," he toasts.

"*Salud,*" I answer, and we take up our spoons.

. . .

AFTER THE RAINS THAT BEGAN THE WEEK, FRIDAY blooms unseasonably warm. Hopefully, far west of here, rings of purple irises are pushing up through the thawing ground.

I lie in bed through a cycle of the snooze alarm, with the windows open a few inches, and listen to someone on the other side of the opaque bottom windows sorting through the recycling bin. When he finishes, he lets the lid drop closed and heads east with his grocery cart of aluminum cans, all shimmying like Lotto balls, and whistles as he goes, pausing his song each time he stops at something of interest. When he eventually rounds the corner at the far end of the street, the still dark morning is silent for a moment.

What do we have? What can I make? The questions are there before I open my eyes. There has been talk lately of how I spend seventy dollars at the market and still we wind up with no meals. We have ingredients, but nothing mutually agreeable seems to come of them. "I feel like I'm the guinea pig, and your future husband is going to reap the rewards," Rich once said, back when our relationship was still young enough that he was game to come over and sample whatever I had tried my hand at in the kitchen. *"You are,"* I'd said, laughing. Wasn't cooking supposed to be the one thing I actually knew how to do—was more decent at than most? Hadn't my mother taught me how to cook and clean and sew (lowered the ironing board for me, all those years ago, so that I could perfectly iron and fold my dolls' clothes), but I was choosing not to have that life? I had said, *No, thank you. I'll take the fifty-fifty route, please.* So where was she now, my suppressed inner housewife, when I needed her? Why was I floundering so embarrassingly—in my career *and* in the kitchen—when these were the few things I was supposed to have figured out?

Rich can see a pile of silver-blue sardines and know just what to do with them, but unless it's a dish I've watched being made countless times, I'm still more comfortable starting from a recipe. He never wants to talk in advance about what to eat, though, so I hold up my end of the agreement and come home from the market with whatever looks good, but with no real plan for it. Since when am I so passive? There must be something that can be done with the cans of corn, cannellini beans, and chickpeas in the lower cabinet, the half-dozen half-empty pasta boxes on the high cabinet's top shelf, the okra in the freezer door, the celery, shallots, chili peppers, and garlic in the crisper. I can hear my sister Maria as a hungry teenager, hanging on the door of my mother's pantry, complaining, "There's no food in here, only . . . *ingredients.*"

I turn off the alarm before it can jump to life again, write for an hour at the kitchen table with a cup of tea (the coffeemaker is too loud with someone sleeping), and shower and dress quietly. Before heading out the door, I walk back to the bed to say goodbye. These days, Rich sits writing at the kitchen table until 2, 2:30, 3 A.M., long after I've gone to sleep.

A step shy of the bed, I pause to take him in. I've always liked the look of Rich sleeping, momentarily relieved of the weight of the world. Although it's too easy to imagine that behind his closed lids the wheels and cogs of his lightning-quick brain still churn. ("*Steel trap*," he'll joke, producing the name, the number, the date that slipped through my sievelike memory years ago.) He's the problem solver in our relationship, among his siblings, with his parents; the go-to person for friends; the colleague people want to work with, to partner with on projects, and he keeps it all in the air—a skinny Atlas—while trying to focus on his own interests as well.

I lean down and put a kiss on his smooth, high cheekbone, and he smiles, eyes still closed, and says, "I love you, have a good day."

Glad he's awake, I lean back in and whisper, "How do you feel about halibut *en papillote*?" I've been reading about how simple it is to steam fish inside parchment paper.

He frowns. "I can't really think about that now," he says, prying open an eye to look at me with new suspicion and pulling the covers more tightly to his chin.

The crowd on the Bedford subway platform seems to grow by the week, and it's becoming more common to have to wait for a second or even a third train before I can squeeze inside; but still I look forward to commuting for the thirty minutes of guilt-free reading time it gives me each way. I make sure to have my book in hand when I step into the train, so that no matter how tightly packed we are—a thing less objectionable in the morning, when the smell of shampoo still comes off some women, more eyes are closed, the agreeable scent of cheap coffee is in the air, and, like a family around the breakfast table, not yet awake enough to argue, we adjust for new hands around the center pole and bounce and rock and lean silently together—I can still pin my elbow to my side and hold my book up under my chin.

As a girl, my favorite gift was to be brought to the bookstore and allowed to pick out a handful of paperbacks. Judy Blume, Beverly Cleary, Paula Danziger—I still have them all, in a box on the high shelf of the coat closet; it's valuable real estate, but I don't want to risk mold by leaving it in my mother's basement. She doesn't know how I can marry an unlike-minded Christian, but I can even less imagine attaching myself to someone who doesn't also pine for an hour alone with a book. She brought my sisters and me to the library twice a week when we were girls, checked out ten books each trip, and read to us until she was hoarse; but on her own she's not a reader. I wish she were. It would be a comfort to know that she was less alone, with so many good people to visit and places to return to. Macondo. Dijon. Florence. How many times, with Frances Mayes, have I enjoyed the wasp that visits her bright Tuscan kitchen each day, for just a quick sip from the faucet? Yes, a good eater, a good reader, and even a Democrat—these are my marriage dealbreakers.

Rising up into the sunlight of Lexington Avenue, from deep below the Citicorp building, the answer to dinner comes to me, like a name recalled: sweet-potato stew! From the cheap vegetarian cookbook with the too-orange photographs. We even have all the ingredients for a simple corn bread to go with it. On my office chair, the magazine's art director has left feature layouts, but my first order of business is to email

Rich my brilliant plan. "All we need is a butternut squash, two sweet potatoes, and a small sour cream. Can you pick those up?" He's out of bed and brewing coffee, and agrees to shop after lunch, motivated by the corn bread.

"You're going to think about this all day now, aren't you," he emails back. Which is true, though I don't exactly know why.

Tonight I skip the gym and Rich offers to help. While I pull ingredients from the cabinets and refrigerator, he puts on a sample wedding dinnertime playlist for me to listen to; our friend Goh has agreed to accompany me down the aisle with his acoustic guitar, but otherwise the music will come courtesy of Rich's white laptop. I open two beers, press on the fold of the paperback cookbook so it stays open, and we clink bottles and divvy up chores. (*This is so fun! Will we always do this?*)

Through tracks of Billie Holiday, Glenn Miller, and Frank Sinatra, I chop onions, garlic, and red chili peppers, and Rich peels the sweet potatoes and the butternut squash. Both will be boiled in salted water—a preparation I loathe, for all the vitamins it sends down the drain—and then chopped and added to the stew pot once everything's simmering: vegetable stock, chopped tomatoes in their juice, onions, garlic, chilies and chili powder, okra, sweet green peppers, canned corn, tomato paste, and cloves. The recipe suggests a side of warmed taco shells but we both prefer the corn bread, and, in keeping with the taco theme, once the stew is plated I like a dollop of sour cream and a sprinkle of chopped cilantro, stems and all.

The corn bread is also my job, and as soon as I turn on the oven the kitchen heats up. We can get a cross breeze if we open the bedroom windows, prop the front door with a shoe, and then open the communal hallway windows. But we're right beside the building's front door, so this puts us on display to everyone coming and going. A few weeks ago, I met a new neighbor in the laundry room who said he'd moved into the corner apartment; when I told him I was the first door beside the entrance, his memory clicked: "Ah, you're sneaker-in-the-door!" I cringed at the realization that we had earned ourselves a nickname, so for now the door stays closed.

Once the corn bread is in the oven I jog back toward the bedroom to adjust the fan, missing something Rich starts to say.

"What's that?" I take a few steps back.

He's standing at the peninsula of countertop, chunking the sweet potatoes on the cutting board. "And these really don't have to be perfect," he says. "You just want to get them more or less the same size so they cook evenly." He looks up with an overly ingratiating smile. "I wish I could tell you how *good* it smells in here!" It takes a beat for me to realize that he's doing a Food Network voice and I'm the audience.

"Thanks, Ming," I say, heading back to the fan.

"Ming's not on that channel anymore," he calls after me. "They don't have *any* ethnic people on that channel!"

An hour later, the kitchen is sweltering and we sit down to an attractive but starch-heavy meal. I planned to make a salad, but in the end everything took so long that I can't be bothered, and, despite two forms of chili, the stew is mysteriously lacking in heat, a needed component to cut through the heft of the vegetables. After a few bites, I get up for the Sriracha chili sauce—a condiment I can't believe I ever lived without, pre-Rich—and we take turns spotting our servings with orange-red dots of it.

"It's not *bad,* though," Rich offers, which makes me laugh. The counters are strewn with evidence of our efforts, I'm stripped to a purple tank top but still sweating, and even Rich, who almost never shows signs of heat, is flushed from stirring at the stove while the corn bread baked. All three bedroom windows are open, the standing fan is on, and still the thermostat says eighty-three. I give in and prop open the door.

Rich takes another Negro Modelo from the refrigerator and splits it between our glasses, and, despite adding to the leaden feeling in my thighs, it tastes like heaven. I press the cold, empty bottle to my cheeks, and we sit digesting what Maria would consider a week's worth of carbohydrates.

"They should make a cooking show where a normal person cooks something and then a chef cooks it and shows them how to improve it," Rich says.

"They should make a cooking show where they tally the cost of all the ingredients at the end," I say. "I love it when they're using fifteen dollars' worth of *mixed fresh herbs.* . . ."

"They should make a show where a chef shows up at your house and has to cook with what you have—"

"They already did that," I say, interrupting him.

"And *then,*" he finishes, "the chef has to make *two other* types of dishes from the leftovers." He sits back, smug.

"That's not bad," I agree.

My phone rings, and seeing that it's Yasmine I answer it on speaker. She and Patrik are living in D.C. this year, where they both found jobs, and on their way home from dinner they've gotten it in their heads that we should drive down for a visit. "Come down, come down!" Yasmine is saying, the two of them talking over each other. "It'll be *so fun!*"

I miss them both so much that for a second it seems worth considering. "Come!" she keeps saying. "Borrow your neighbor's car—you can be here by midnight!" I wish my bag was packed by the door, that the kitchen wasn't in need of an exhaustive cleanup, and, most of all, that Rich weren't leaving for a business trip in the morning, which really settles it.

"I wish we were there," Patrik says when we tell them we're at the table, that we've turned the apartment into a sauna, that Rich wants to install a screen door. "I miss our dinners in 9J," he adds, and we all agree. Though, of course, it was just months ago that we were dying to leave that apartment behind and be done with its grim inner-courtyard view, the scalding pipe beside the shower, and the night doorman, Tim, who would make Rich and Patrik sign the ledger each time, acting as though he didn't know them.

Yasmine blows kisses through the phone. "I have my dress all picked out," she says before we hang up. "I can't wait for this wedding—my first real American wedding! Only twelve more weeks!"

Can it really be so soon? Twelve weeks, and then what's done is done. Twelve weeks and I'll be sealed to a man who's willing to spend his Friday night chopping vegetables when I feel the frugal urge to use up frozen okra and canned corn.

. . .

WE HAVE A NICE Saturday morning with Americanos, scrambled eggs, and NPR on the radio, and then Rich is off to Los Angeles for three days. I do some writing, go to the gym, do laundry, and keep the radio on to prevent the apartment from feeling empty. Before meeting friends at a party tonight, I make a salad of mesclun, English cucumber, and olives, and then tear up and toss in the last few inches of the baguette we had with breakfast, which sat on the counter all day wrapped in one of the pretty red cloth napkins I bought the day we moved in. Red-onion slices would complete this nicely, but I'd rather not be remembered for them later at the party.

Picking through the salad, I think again about the napkins and the morning of the move. We'd woken up in Rich's old apartment, a cute three hundred square feet with a window seat and a step up to the bathroom, and had stayed in bed past the alarm, listening to the sounds of the neighborhood for the last time: an exuberant bird on the tree limb reaching toward the window, the reverberating *bong* announcing the half hour in the cupola of the stone church on the corner, where men would already be in line for free coffee, and later Rafi, the dry cleaner, sweeping the sidewalk below us with a corn broom—*shoosh, shoosh, shoosh*—a sound that delivers me back to the summer after second grade, listening to my father clear the mess of a tall mimosa tree off our back patio. Its flowers would soon get it cut down.

How much longer would we have lain there, had we known that the morning sounds in our new ground-floor apartment would be the city's fleet of street sweepers roaring off from their nearby storage site, the blaring radio of the woman delivering newspapers in the dark of 5 A.M., and the stream of regulars sifting through cascades of glass and aluminum cans in the recycling bins? Some mornings I want to save them the trouble and shout from my pillow, "You're too late! Four people have been through it already!"

The moving truck was scheduled to be at my apartment

at noon, and then head the two miles south to Rich's. After a quick breakfast down the street, he headed back upstairs to finish packing and I started uptown on foot, wanting to stop at a particular bakery for doughnuts for Eddie, the doorman, whom I was going to miss, and Alex, the maintenance manager, who had agreed to run the freight elevator for the moving men. It was warming up quickly, though, and I was beginning to regret my choice of bakery and the decision to walk when I passed a shop with pretty linens in the window and, in the market for a shower curtain, went inside. They didn't have shower curtains, but on an end table piles of polished-cotton napkins were on sale. They were fresh and bright, and the price was good, but I didn't *need* them. And in Manhattan—where my bottom dresser drawer had long served as my linen closet, and it no longer seemed ridiculous that Yasmine and I could fit every piece of our tableware (cups, mugs, wineglasses, dinner plates, cereal bowls) behind a single cupboard door—necessity had become my shopping criterion. Plus, Rich and I were already worried that our things might not fit inside the truck I'd ordered; it was easy to imagine exactly the cranky tone he would use if he knew that while he was packing and stressing I was shopping. My new magazine job paid poorly, and between the move, the security deposit, and the reality of being a student in New York City, my bank account had been wiped clean.

Still, I stood there with the napkins.

I was twenty-eight years old, engaged to be married, and moving into—what was in theory, anyway—my first grown-up apartment, and all I had to my name in the way of tableware were six secondhand place mats and a white tablecloth with a red-wine stain. I thought about my non-city-dwelling friends and their exotic *spare bedrooms* and *dining-room sets*. Surely I was entitled to six high-thread-count cotton napkins.

I chose three blue with red tulips and yellow accents and three red with yellow tulips and blue accents and then decided not to tell Rich, which raised a flag in my mind even as I thought it. *Don't tell your father* was a mantra of my childhood. We would leave shopping bags in the trunk of my mother's car until my father left for work the next morning, so that he wouldn't yell about the money we'd spent. Was this marriage? Would Rich really yell?

The smooth cotton of the napkins was so cool I wanted to press one to my cheek. I handed a credit card to the saleswoman, she wrapped the napkins in pink tissue, and, back in my apartment, I tucked them into an untaped box, never mentioning it to Rich. I know perfectly well that My Father doesn't represent All Husbands, and still the association comes instantaneously, as uncontrollable as a flinch.

Tonight, when Rich calls from Los Angeles to say good night, I have a few drinks in me from the party, and before we hang up I say, "You know those red and blue cloth napkins we have? I bought them the morning we moved, on the walk up to my place."

"Oh," he says, not knowing where this is coming from. "Those are nice."

"They were on sale," I offer.

"Oh, well done!" he says, congratulatorily. And then, after a pause to see if we're done with that, "Good night, my baby."

"Good night."

...

"DINNER ALONE is one of life's pleasures," Laurie Colwin wrote in "Alone in the Kitchen with an Eggplant," a perfect essay, in my opinion. "Certainly cooking for oneself reveals man at his weirdest," she continued. "People lie when you ask them what they eat when they are alone. A salad, they tell you. But when you persist, they confess to peanut butter and bacon sandwiches deep fried and eaten with hot sauce, or spaghetti with butter and grape jam."

Colwin made a ritual of eating alone, a thing partly necessitated by her teeny Greenwich Village apartment, which, at seven feet by twenty, the high ceilings alone, she wrote, prevented it from feeling like the inside of a box of animal crackers. On her two-burner hot plate she would stir up a dish of eggplant—fried or stewed, crisp, sludgy, hot or cold—and eat it from a chipped Meissen dish at her child-size desk while watching the national news. (The local news she watched with coffee while getting dinner started.)

Alone in the kitchen, my rituals tend toward standing in my still sweaty gym clothes at the cutting board, sawing slices from a softball-size fresh mozzarella until it's nearer to a golf ball, and then hurriedly rewrapping it and heading to the shower. Later, this is usually followed by a guilty bowl of cereal.

When I do cook, I bother less. I'm happy with an egg and a salad, drizzled with oil and vinegar that can blend or not blend, or eggs and diced zucchini—a soft, one-pot meal that Rich is not overly fond of. Or I'll give in to my love of mushy foods—orzo, pastina, cream of wheat, rice pudding; anything with a subtle texture that can be pressed to the roof of

the mouth and investigated with the tongue. Heaven is a tapi-
oca pudding with plump, distinguishable pearls.

One summer, I worked in the kitchen of a convalescent
center, making puddings and gelatins for its elderly residents.
I'd mark each cup with a sticker to match to their dining re-
strictions: low-fat, no sugar, full purée. I was nineteen and,
crossing the parking lot after my shift in my all-white uniform, I'd gulp lungfuls of air, feeling young and free, my
night just beginning as theirs slowed to a close. Still, making
those puddings, it was a consolation to know that I might
someday be a contented old toothless person.

Guiltiest pleasure of all, alone I'll take my dinner, sidle up
to the television (a thirteen-inch Trinitron, making the sidling
a not unimportant part of this), and let my brain activity slow
to a blip. I watch shows that Rich wouldn't dream of stopping
at and movies with dialogue so abysmal I would deny any
knowledge of them to the few people I know who delight in in-
serting into conversations, "Oh, I don't *have* a television. . . ."

Yasmine shares my affinities for bad television and mushy
foods, though for her the appeal of the latter isn't subtlety of
texture but a funny desire to chew as little as possible. During
our years in 9J, we consumed countless bowls of curried red
lentils over basmati rice while slumped into our old blue
couch watching IQ-dimming teen dramas. That we could
share what I otherwise considered to be a private ritual was
made possible, I imagine, by the fact that Yasmine is naturally
thin and lovely and has seemingly zero qualms about food or
her body, which perhaps partly stems from her having lived,
as the daughter of a diplomat, in countries where food is less
abundant and people's relationships with it are more straightforward. I've spent a decade intentionally leaving two bites

on my plate, but here was a woman who, if I didn't get up for third helpings, would insist with genuine concern, "Why aren't you eating well?"

A. J. Liebling, as a young man in Paris, ate well and alone often, which dispensed him, he wrote, "from defending my whims." And while he managed this in a number of glamorous restaurants, it's at home alone in front of the television that I allow my less attractive whims to play out. Without Rich, I'll have the slice of cake, or the extra serving, I likely wouldn't with him around. No doubt there's some good, old-fashioned self-consciousness at the root of this. My mother has dieted through most of my life and hers, and I inherited her plump thighs and their attendant insecurities. For a few slim years during my early twenties, I experienced shame-free bathing-suit wearing, but now I'm ten pounds heavier and have more or less come to terms with trading a more jiggly bottom half for getting to eat the things I only pined for then. Only my father had a metabolism that burned through whatever he gave it and the long, thin legs that, as a household of women dieters, we all wished for, though this made him an unsympathetic critic of my mother's figure.

There was a night toward the end of their marriage that stays with me. It started off badly, when, washing up after work, he shouted about the hand towels in the bathroom being too small, and from there the mood in the house went tense. Later, at the table, he made a comment about what my mother was eating, or her portion maybe, and suddenly she was on her feet—startling us all, her chair falling backward behind her—spitting the food from her mouth out onto the floor. "Are you happy now?" she screamed, her face contorted with sobs. "Are you happy?" She ran up the stairs to her bedroom, and my sisters, one by one, followed. But, strangely, I stayed. She had surprised him, and sitting there, mouth open, he looked shocked and somehow innocent, and I felt bad to leave him sitting there alone.

"You become one parent and you marry the other," I've heard people say, and, remembering nights like that, I wonder who I'm marrying and who I'm becoming; and when does it become possible to break the pattern and embrace a new option.

Tonight, determined not to sink into the couch with a deep bowl of carbohydrates, I chop a zucchini, shiitakes, scallions, chilies, a few stems of spinach, and some tofu, with a plan to eat them as a soup over half a serving of udon. Once it's all simmering in the pot, though, I can't figure out how to make the broth taste the way it does when Rich makes it. I add more soy sauce, sesame oil, fish oil, but the flavor never materializes.

"I'm eating bad soups over here," I tell him later, lying in bed with the kitchen light on. "You'd better come home right away."

"I'll be home before you can even miss me," he says.

"It's too late for that."

. . .

BRIDGET CALLS ME at the office almost every morning now, for a quick wedding debriefing. They're efficient calls and we stay on topic, which I've come to see is part of their appeal; our energies are reined in, focused together on the same thing, which there has rarely ever been a need for. She calls with a list of questions, and I'll have a question or two for her waiting in the margin of my planner. "Do I want the glass votive holders on sale at the dollar store? Do I want the glass carafes at Walmart? The vases at Target? Do I have ribbon? Do I need poster board? Do I want her to visit the restaurant where we might hold the rehearsal dinner? It's the most we've ever spoken as adults, and even while it's going on I know I'm going to miss it once it's over.

Tonight my key is in the deadbolt when I hear the phone start to ring. "Did I catch you during dinner?" my mother asks. "What are you having?"

"No, I'm just walking in from the gym—"

"At this hour, in the dark!"

"Mom, it's seven-thirty. There are a million people outside."

"You girls make me so worried. . . . Don't you watch the *news*?"

I change the topic. "We made a nice stew the other night, so I'll probably just heat that up. Rich's in L.A. until Tuesday."

"It's just you?" she asks, new worry in her voice. "Are you afraid? Do you want to come stay with me?" This one is actually my fault. While my sisters and I pride ourselves on being the type of women to call when you need a sofa moved up a stairwell, when it comes to sleeping alone it's a too-well-known fact that my bravado crumbles. I wake three, four times a night in a sweat, dreaming that there are ghosts standing over the bed.

"No, but thanks. I've been experimenting with leaving different lights on." Then, wanting to tell someone this, and thinking she might like my confiding in her, I offer, "It's kind of nice, though, to be alone and eat what I want. It's such a pain to figure out what we both feel like eating each night."

"You're asking him what he *wants*?" she says, her voice rising. "Why are you asking him what he wants? You're not a restaurant. Just make something. I never asked your father what he wanted. He just ate whatever I made."

"Mom, he's not a *dog*," I say, my tone suddenly the irritated one I too easily fall into with her lately. "I don't just put food down and expect him to eat it. He's a grown person. Nobody wants to eat food they don't feel like eating. You know you'd rather eat something you feel like eating." As soon as I stop, I feel a slap of guilt for snapping at her. "I mean, it's not *hard*," I say more gently. "It's just weird to have to think about it."

My father's mother infamously averted this problem by cooking on a regimen: Sunday, pasta with meatballs or braciole, with its toothpicks to look out for. Monday, chicken. Tuesday, a soup with a seasonal vegetable and either lentils or leftover chicken if there was any. Wednesday was macaroni with string beans or broccoli rabe. Thursdays, a frittata. Friday, as with most Catholics, fish, and on Saturdays came the spoil of a steak or a roast. The first week that my parents were married my father said, "It's Tuesday—where's the soup?"

"W-*ell*," my mother says, rustled by my tone but moving past it. "I just think the best-tasting meals are those that someone else makes for you. I don't think your father ever cooked for me once. Rich should be happy someone else is willing to do the work."

When we hang up, I make a halfhearted quesadilla with Fontina, a jalapeño, and the last of the tortillas I intended to use for breakfast burritos. Then, deeply installed in the couch, I finish my night of carbs with the last of the sweet-potato stew, followed by one juicy tangerine.

. . .

A LIGHT DINNER of baby spinach and an omelet with the *Gilmore Girls* tonight, while waiting for groceries to be delivered. I've been thinking about how, if we cook for others as a way of caring for them—which most people agree that we do—then what does it mean when we cook, or don't cook, for ourselves? Does the act revert to being solely about sustenance? And is that really so bad? As satisfying as a good meal is, sometimes it's even nicer to be eating within five minutes of walking through the door, and to have only a dirty spatula and a skillet in the sink. Maybe elaborate meals are more fun when there's someone to share the excitement (and the dirty dishes) with. Or maybe—and I think this is it—the ways that I love others are just different from the ways that I go about caring for myself.

Rich's flight tomorrow should put him through the door near dinnertime, and I decide to make him a special homecoming meal. I pile my favorite cookbooks around me on the couch and mark pages with Post-its. *Meat-free for me, filling for him, not a lot of dishes . . .* Pappardelle with Mushroom, Wine, and Herbs? Red Lentil Soup with Lime? Polenta Gratin with Mushrooms and Tomato? Eventually, I decide on the slightly exotic-sounding Hot & Sour Pumpkin Soup from *The Gourmet Cookbook,* which I'll serve with a watercress and mandarin-orange salad, and a cauliflower gratin. For dessert, I'll pick up a few inches of the odd Jell-O cake he likes (alternating layers of yellow cake and cream with red and green

Jell-O cubes suspended in it) from the Polish bakery. I'm excited to get started, and I write out a careful grocery list of items I'll need to pick up after work tomorrow and tuck it into my wallet so there's no chance of forgetting it.

Ten minutes before ten, the delivery person arrives and drops my boxes of groceries between the living room and the kitchen. When he discreetly glances over the apartment while I sign his clipboard, I'm relieved to realize I had changed the channel, during a commercial, to *Voyage of Endurance,* a documentary about Ernest Shackleton.

. . .

I WASTE AN HOUR in the dark after work searching the Indian shops around Twenty-eighth Street for galangal and Kaffir leaves. I find neither (which I discover, too late, is because both are Thai), but it's a consolation to leave with incredibly cheap cellophane packets of pine nuts, pungent chili powder, and sesame seeds. I remember to buy wine, which I overlooked last night, but then forgot to stop for the cake.

Once the soup is simmering, I add lime juice in place of the Kaffir leaves. (Having no idea what galangal tastes like, I simply ignore those instructions.) Still, the final taste can hardly be called exotic. The gratin, too—a recipe from my Aunt Teresa, written on a notecard in her tidy hand—is underwhelming. Not enough butter? Should I have mashed the cauliflower more? It turns out flat and lifeless and not worth smelling up the kitchen for. Why didn't I make the pappardelle with mushrooms?

Rich's flight is delayed, and he drags himself through the door past nine. We have an awkward meal—me peppering him with questions and him tired from a day of travel and a bumpy flight and, I again realize too late, wishing he were sitting alone to "re-combobulate," as he likes to say.

Cleaning up together afterward, he gets cranky and snaps that it doesn't make sense to spend twenty dollars on ingredients when we could have spent the same amount on takeout, not had to clean up, and gotten more work done.

"It was a homecoming meal," I tell him, feeling my cheeks go hot with embarrassment. Then he feels bad and apologizes and says again how good it was, though really it was just okay.

Now we've gone our separate ways, him to the couch with his laptop and me to my closet and my journal, after I type what we ate into the Word document I've been keeping; when I studied anthropology in college, I liked that the details of every day, compiled, became data to study and draw conclusions from. Once the honeymoon of those summer months was over, and the repetition of dinner inched from a delight to a chore, it occurred to me that the choices we're making each night, compiled, would surely say something about us—illuminate even the smallest part of this great unknown ahead of us—and I want to know what that is.

Rich's and my first big trip together was to Switzerland. It was only my second time abroad, and traveling such a distance together made our relationship feel suddenly more serious and grown-up. "We are over the Labrador Sea!" I had jotted in the back of the book I was reading, our dinner trays cleared, the lights dimmed, and everyone settling in for the night. I had never heard of this sea before, but there I was flying over it, my exact whereabouts known only to Rich, who sat beside me reading and holding my hand, managing to turn the pages without letting go. We were on an adventure, just the two of us! It was an excellent trip, but what came back to me, as I typed in my list and tried to make sense of his mood, was the relief of having him leave me, afterward, in front of my Los Angeles apartment—him offering to carry up my bags and me insisting no, just wanting him to drive off so that I could finally be alone. Then, unpacking in my room with the door closed, carrying in a bowl of cereal to eat on my bed, and not wanting even the intrusion of the radio. It's one thing to know how to be together, and it's another to learn when to be apart.

YASMINE-STYLE LENTILS

> 1 cup red lentils
> 1 tablespoon butter or vegetable oil
> Salt to taste
> 1 teaspoon cumin
> 1 teaspoon chili powder
> ½ teaspoon turmeric
> 1 teaspoon minced garlic
> 1 teaspoon minced ginger

WHEN YOU ARE HOME ALONE, make a few servings of white rice—basmati is preferable. If you don't feel like washing the rice cooker, or you're not great at measuring a perfect rice-to-water ratio, cook the rice in a big pot of boiling water, strain it, and return it to the hot pot to further dry out. (You are home alone; no one needs to know.)

Put a cup of red lentils into a saucepan. (Don't be tempted to use the rugged brown ones, which have a grittiness and stay solid; the red lentils break down to almost a purée.) Rinse them in the pot until the water stops being cloudy. (You could use a fine-mesh colander, but then you'll have to wash it.) Cover the lentils with cold water about an inch above the lentils and bring this to a boil. Scoop out any scummy foam that forms on top, trying not to spill any on the countertop or stove; it's very nearly glue, and a pain to clean up. Lower the heat to medium and add the butter or vegetable oil, a good teaspoon of salt, and the cumin, chili powder, turmeric, garlic, and ginger (these last two can be fresh or minced from a jar). Stir this, leaving the heat on medium-low so the lentils simmer gently, and then cover partially.

Next, lie on the couch and watch a television program that the person you live with, but who is not home now, thinks is stupid and always clicks past. Every now and then, get up and stir the lentils, preventing them from sticking to the bottom of the pot. When the water has been absorbed, add some more until the lentils reach a consistency you like, whether that's soupy or thick enough to stand a spoon in. After 20 to 30 minutes, they'll be slowly popping and churning around in the pot with a baby-food-like consistency, and it's ready, though you can also keep adding water and let it reduce for another 20 or 30 minutes, if you really want the spices to come together and mellow out. Add more salt to taste (you'll likely need more than you think). If a green vegetable seems like a good idea, and you have a prewashed bag of spinach, throw some on top of the finished rice with a sprinkle of salt and cover it for a minute until wilted. No need to dirty a skillet. A sliced, salted cucumber on the side is another, maybe even better, idea.

Put a few big scoops of rice into a bowl. Add the lentils over the rice or beside it, whichever you prefer, and then lay the spinach where you'd like it. (This is all about you, after all.) Return to the couch and watch more television. Eat, refill your bowl, repeat. Refuse to feel guilty.

⋯

I T'S AN EARLY MARCH DAY OF GRAY SKIES, AND AFTER a work meeting in Union Square I treat myself to a walk through the farmers' market. I'm craving something juicy and hydrating, but the stalls are filled with apples and more apples, all looking small and dull in their crates. Long gone are the blushing Galas and Honeycrisps of early October, their cider scent reaching the nose from several steps back. Even the roses for sale nearby—the banner pinned beneath the table urging MAKE SOMEONE HAPPY! $20/DOZ.—are barely enticing, their pale-pink buds wrapped tight as little fists. These are days to envy those patient souls who have mastered the trick of canning and still have tomatoes and yellow peaches enough to last until spring.

The organized side of me thrills to the idea of an old-fashioned, well-appointed pantry with hand-dated jars, but there's more to it, something deeper down. When M.F.K. Fisher lived in Switzerland with her second husband, she stocked their cellar with the fruits from their hillside. "When I went down into the coolness and saw all the things sitting

there so richly quiet on the shelves," she wrote, "I had a special feeling of contentment. It was a reassurance of safety
against hunger, very primitive and satisfying."

The pleasure of a well-stocked pantry seems to me some
combination of frugality, comfort, and possibility. I'd love a
shelf of penny-candy jars filled with dried fruits, lentils, rice,
oats—an image with roots back to Mr. Olsen's tidy mercan-
tile in *Little House on the Prairie.* Though, the greatest pantry I
can imagine is the one Marcel Boulestin describes in his
memoir, *Myself, My Two Countries.* Boulestin was a French
chef with a long affinity for the British, and his grandmother,
in the Périgord, kept the type of living pantry where everything was of the moment, edging toward a decay averted
only by the resourcefulness of its owner. He wrote:

> In the store room next to the kitchen were a long
> table and shelves always covered with all sorts of pro-
> visions; large earthenware jars full of confits of pork
> and goose, a small barrel where vinegar slowly ma-
> tured, a bowl where honey oozed out of the comb,
> jams, preserves of sorrel and of tomatoes, and odd
> bottles with grapes and cherries marinating in
> brandy; next to the table a weighing machine on
> which I used to stand at regular intervals; sacks of
> haricot beans, of potatoes; eggs, each one carefully
> dated in pencil.
>
> And there were the baskets of fruit, perfect small
> melons, late plums, under-ripe medlars waiting to
> soften, peaches, pears hollowed out by a bird or a
> wasp, figs that had fallen of their own accord, all the

fruits of September naturally ripe and sometimes still warm from the sun. Everything in profusion.

I had to look up what a medlar is, but I was well rewarded. It's a small, buttocks-shaped fruit that must be left to wrinkle and soften before it can be served with cheese or made into jam or wine. Its shape, of course, and quality of "not being ripe until it's rotten" inspired bawdy jokes throughout literature, and Shakespeare and Chaucer did their part to secure the poor medlar as a symbol of prostitution.

There's an appeal, as well, in such profusion. My father always kept a garden, and after he left I kept the tradition going, turning the soil each spring and starting from seedlings. I've realized it's a different feeling now to buy zucchinis for a bread than it was to bake one as a way of working through the glut the garden left us with, even after bags of them had been carried to the neighbors. Always, after the sprawling plants seemed to have run their course, there would be a final beast to discover—long and curving like a swan's neck, or straight and thick as a baseball bat—hiding under the low, wide leaves and entwined in their prickly stems.

Today's market is an abbreviated one. There are grape-vine wreaths and dried flowers, honeys and jams, the bakery stand with its pies and wood-framed breadboxes, a fishmonger, whose pricey, white offerings—shrimp, flounder, scallops—were surely more attractive on fresh ice this morning. Even in the large vegetable stall, where piles of leeks, thick as wrists, have their sandy roots turned toward the crowd, and the blousy chard are piled high, nothing calls to me. Still, not wanting to leave empty-handed, I buy a bunch of lacinato kale, liking its prehistoric-looking, vitamin-rich leaves, and that—no sand or floppy leaves here—it's small enough to fit into my oversized bag. No reason, after all, to alert the rest of the office to my detour.

Preparedness seems to be a theme this week. Last night my editor, leaving the office with a guitar case slung over his shoulder, sent me, with seventy or so other journalists, to the launch party for a new cellphone at an Asian-fusion restaurant in SoHo. For an hour we mingled, exchanged business cards, stared at the waterfall splashing into a koi pond when the small talk dried up, and drank specially mixed cocktails that played off the cellphone's name. When finally we were told to find our seats, speeches were made, applause was offered, and an anxious line of waiters were freed to race their covered trays to each table. Which is the part of these evenings that I look forward to most, since it's when the conversation tends to turn to more general topics.

When a young guy across the table pulled up photos of his new baby, the conversation, to my great relief, moved from bandwidth to marriage, and I asked the handsome strawberry blonde seated beside me—a Brit who had already offered that he had a wife and a dog but no kids—who did the cooking in his house. This was maybe overly brazen, but the question weighs heavy on me these days.

He smiled for a moment, gauging whether I was serious, and then answered, "We both do. Though more often I do."

"What do you make?"

"It depends what's in the larder," he said. "It's *critical* to keep a stocked larder." Which is nothing I ever would have disagreed with, but when he said it, the truth of it newly struck me. Day-to-day shopping is always preferable, however inconvenient it can be, but that's exactly the point of a good pantry: it's the fail-safe.

His accent also instantly converted me to the appeal of larder over pantry. Where *pantry* is puritanical, nonperishable (the Mr. Olsen's dry goods of my fantasy), *larder* evokes its roots as a place for wines or meats—richer foods— and their fermentation, fecundity. Although the Brit said that he mostly stocks his larder with tins of fish, pasta, *canned veg,* milk powder, and chicken and beef stocks. Often, he added, they'll have "cauliflower-cheese," which seemed essentially a gratin—steamed cauliflower covered with béchamel sauce.

"And it doesn't have to be cauliflower," he continued, warming to the topic. "You can eat just about anything that way. Broccoli, aubergines . . ." It sounded good to me, though I struggled to imagine Rich, my clean-flavors advocate, agreeing to a bubbly casserole of cheese sauce.

Still, the handsome Brit has inspired me to want to fortify our skinny pantry cabinet—stuffed to the gills with wellintended but useless items—into more of a kitchen ally, and within a half hour of arriving home I'm on my knees beside the stove, pulling items from its depths.

"When did we get hoisin sauce?" I ask, but Rich has retreated back to the bed with his laptop and headphones, and no answer comes. There's a large tin of dolmades, the Greekstyle stuffed grape leaves, that Rich found in a Polish bodega and thought looked interesting. A can of coconut milk, which I will one day figure out how to cook with. Rice flour that Rich bought for making crêpes, though he never has. And a can of pickled Chinese turnip greens that his mother gave us, along with an empty jam jar for storing the leftovers, which she insisted we'd definitely have.

When we visited his parents in Boston this summer, his older sister's bedroom had been prepared for me, complete with new house slippers beside the bed. (In both our parents' homes, we are still given separate rooms, the unspoken message being *engaged is still not married.*) There were also several paper grocery bags lined up along the wall. "I know it's difficult for you people to carry home heavy things from the market," she explained, "so I bought some things for you to bring back in the car."

In the bags were oil and vinegar, cans of stock, thick jars of cornichons, and a few smaller glass jars protectively wrapped in newspaper. When we unwrapped them at home, we found bulbous jars of ghostly white pickled scallion bulbs, stackable canisters of shredded brown fish powder, and slim jars of inch-long silver fish covered in golden chili oil, their wide-open eyes as black and lifeless as pencil lead. They're all condiments for fried rice and congee, with which small plates of pickled or salty garnishes are offered for contrast and extra flavor. We've visited twice more since then, and each time the paper grocery bags have been waiting.

I move all but one of the scallion bulbs, silver fish, and brown fish powder to the immensely inconvenient cabinet above the refrigerator, along with all the other items I have no immediate or imaginable use for. When I'm finished, it's hardly a room of ripening fruits and hand-dated eggs, but it's a start.

Rich has been encouraging me to strike out sans recipe, and now I look over the two pared-down shelves for inspiration. There's a jar of gourmet pesto that his older sister put in his Christmas stocking, and a can of cannellini beans, and I work from there, putting on a pot of salted water for rigatoni and then sautéing the washed and chopped kale with garlic, white wine, lemon juice, red-pepper flakes, and salt and pepper. When it's tender, I add the drained and rinsed beans, and, once they're warm add in the rigatoni, already tossed through with the pesto. To finish, each plate gets a blanket of Argentine Parmesan on the microplaner instead of the grater (a tip from a Gordon Ramsay program), which turns the cheese into a wonderful textural element, billowy and quick-dissolving as snowflakes.

Rich is more proud of my improvisation than he is unhappy about the kale, which he finds chewy and I find uniquely savory. The best thing about the kale, though, was washing it and watching the way the water ran across the textured undersides of each leaf; some trick of physics made the water coagulate and look like dozens of diamonds, or tiny glass marbles, tumbling inside the curved pockets of each leaf. When I called Rich over to look, he stood beside me at the sink for longer than I expected, equally mesmerized.

. . .

PITTS SHARES ITS block with five restaurants, three bars, three furniture stores, a high-end men's clothing shop, a record store, and a place that each day rolls out a rack of used baby clothing—the tiny offerings hanging so high on the silver bar that the rack's exposed legs appear almost immodest. But the street's aesthetic—and scent—is undoubtedly set by the meat distributor, whose sidewalks are often slick with a dark stain that drives the flies wild. Negotiating these few slippery yards, hosed down each evening by the man who will impatiently pause to let me pass, feels a fitting prelude to the Pitts's grocery-shopping experience. Severed fish heads reliably wait on ice, and half a dozen Belgian beers are stocked in a giant cold room, but often there isn't a single half-quart of skim milk, or any bread, or the Jif peanut butter will fall out of inventory for a season. When I find it on the bottom shelf, I buy two.

Yesterday I caught it at a good time, though, and the shelves were full. I bought baby arugula, a small ricotta, and a bunch of organic spinach, still rhubarb-pink at its roots, for a baked ziti and salad, and then two fillets of skate, a tomato on the vine, and two skinny organic zucchini to cook in parchment paper. Trying for a third dinner, I collected Swiss chard, a skirt steak, and a block of firm tofu; when Rich has time to make the steak for himself, I'll herb-encrust the tofu for me and we can both have the chard and rice, or maybe polenta.

In the produce area, a chilly room in the back, I paused over a squeaky foursome of organic scallions. Rich likes to add them to a steak marinade with soy sauce, brown sugar, ginger, garlic, and gin. "You're not really hesitating over $1.69. . . ." I could hear him deadpanning in my ear, but I was. It annoys me to work at a job I don't like in order to earn money to buy and throw away these high-maintenance vegetables, which beat even the organic milk in their insistence on spoiling within twenty-four hours of entering the house.

If I forgo the clear plastic produce bag in the name of environmental do-goodism, the scallions will let their taut tops wilt down and shrivel that night. If I agree to put them in a plastic bag but then twist the top of the bag at all securely, they turn slimy. To satisfy the scallions, there must be a bag; the bag must be completely dry, which means drying the scallions that were made damp by the grocery-store mister; a paper towel must accompany them back inside the bag; and the top of the bag must be ever so slightly folded over, as though one accidentally brushed against a bag that was otherwise open and breezy. And even then there's no guarantee.

I grabbed a plastic bag, put the scallions in my basket, and headed to the register.

At home I put the fish in the freezer and the steak in the refrigerator, to make that night. But after the gym I was too tired to cook, and Rich was working on a deadline, so we ordered in, making the meat a must-have for the next day. But this morning a friend emailed inviting us to a last-minute birthday dinner, which started me wondering about the steak: How many days can it sit there, chilled but defrosted? And what kind of people allow their social life to be dictated by six dollars' worth of raw meat? We go to the party, and when we get home I throw away the meat and replace the damp paper towel in the scallion bag.

"I can't believe how stressful it is to keep scallions alive," I tell Rich, getting into bed.

"Oh, don't worry," he offers reassuringly. "My mother has been stressing about scallions her entire life."

I look up to see if he's joking, but he's pulling a clean T-shirt over his head before getting into bed. "Well, at least we know what to look forward to," I say, eyes closed on the pillow and not wanting to join that club alone.

W HEN I PASS THROUGH THE KITCHEN AFTER A SHOWER, my damp gym clothes balled under my arm, the rice cooker is bubbling away with its nutty scent, and Rich is at work on a stir-fry with shrimp and sugar-snap peas. He finished an assignment early today and offered to take over dinner.

When he cooks, he's all confidence and contentment, and chopping garlic at the cutting board now he whistles a line from "Get Me to the Church on Time." (His mother used to play a cassette of *My Fair Lady* in the car on long road trips.) Then, unable to resist the Cockney accent, he half sings it to me as well, more gutturally than even Alfred Doolittle managed.

He's happy, too, that with Chinese food neither of us expects to eat a salad. Italians are big salad eaters and, growing up, making a salad was as normal a part of being asked to set the table as folding napkins or putting out a carafe of wine for my father. Rich is coming around to the idea, though at first he found it unfathomable. "I can't believe that I'm going to face salad, every night, for the rest of my life," he remarked one night, punctuating his words with dramatic pauses. We have spinach, baby spinach, arugula, mesclun, dandelions, baby field greens. On the nights that we're most rushed, a salad is greens in a vinaigrette with a grating of Parmesan or Pecorino at the table, but more often I include a fruit, a cheese, toasted nuts or seeds; sometimes I even candy the pecans or walnuts, which he loves. This is hardly a man choking down heads of iceberg lettuce. And still, most nights he pulls the salad plate toward him like it's a chore.

During our Christmas visit with his family, he brought up our salad conversations over dinner, and everyone had laughed. "Chinese people don't really like salad," his younger sister, Alexandra, explained.

"One time, we were at the house of one of Babah's colleagues," his mother chimed in. She is a very cute storyteller. She sits up straight and elongates her neck like Audrey Hepburn, her black bob hitting a neat point at her jaw. "They served salad, and Babah said, 'Oh, the salad is so *good!*' and he ate it all up. So I thought, Oh, Babah likes salad. So that week I made salad at home. And he said, 'Salad! What are you making salad for? I hate salad!' And I said, 'But you liked it at your friend's house.'"

We turned our heads to Rich's father at the opposite end of the table. He has a gentle manner, a mischievousness in his eyes, and a soft salt-and-pepper buzz cut that Rich will no doubt someday mimic. "I was just being polite," he said with a slow grin. And everyone laughed again.

I steal a crisp pod from the silver colander in the sink and walk back to stare at the clothes in my closet. "Am I never going to see you in real clothes again?" Rich teased the other day. I leave for work as he's waking up, change for the gym when I get home, shower before dinner, and then . . . It's 8 P.M. on a weekday—can't I put on pajamas? We're just going to eat, maybe watch TV, read, work at our computers. Every woman I've ever lived with, within minutes of arriving home, has traded constricting pants or dry-clean-only clothing, even jeans, for pajama bottoms or knockaround pants— a term I appropriated in college for the drawstring or elastic-waist cotton, or sometimes flannel, pants we wore around the apartment and sometimes beyond it, in order to absolve them of pajama status. Is it so lazy not to want to create a fourth set of clothes for the day (work clothes, gym clothes, pajamas, and dinner clothes)? Or does all this hint of *letting myself go,* the well-acknowledged beginning of the marital end, before the wedding has even occurred? All this comes, too, on top of the strangeness of not having another woman around; for the first time in my life, I have only my own clothes to wear.

I settle on pajama bottoms (cotton, not flannel, and more yoga pant than knockaround), with a T-shirt and bra. At least the parts he sees across the table will look normal.

Rich is at the sink, peeling shrimp. "Do you need help?"

"Nope, I'm fine," he says, in a tone that implies that he doesn't want me underfoot, peering under his pot lids. "You just go relax."

I sometimes like to call my mother on the nights that Rich cooks. As a practical matter, it gives me an extra thirty minutes I wouldn't otherwise have; but when she asks how Rich is I also get to say, with a feigned nonchalance that I surprise even myself with, "He's fine—he's making dinner."

"Oh, good boy! Tell him I'm proud of him!" she'll respond satisfyingly. The women in my family have certain expectations of men, and any failure or lethargy on a man's part to meet these rarely goes unnoticed. But cooking is fully bonus-points territory.

My mother served dinner at five-thirty each evening, as part of a routine choreographed around my father's arrival. In our home, the person coming and going kissed everyone hello and goodbye, but when we heard our father's key in the door my sisters and I knew to leave what we were doing and go to him instead. Like dinner waiting for him, this gesture of respect was something he expected from us. He had a quick temper that we knew to avoid, but when all was calm we thoroughly enjoyed one another. He built us a jungle gym from old ladders, and in his sticky-fingered way he brought home for us whatever he came across—rabbits, baby chicks, a turtle (a snapper, it turned out, which was quickly re-released)—and would play tag with us and wrestle in the living room, eventually surrendering to his three daughters, like a Gulliver pinned down by so many Lilliputian strings.

After dinner, our plates cleared, we'd rush to his lap and compete for his attention. He sat in the corner and would push back his chair so that it grazed the two walls and one of us could stand on its thick backrest (it was a padded metal square and we were kids, made of fluff), and in this way he accommodated our three bodies. While our mother cleared the table and reset it with fruit, nuts, and a gold-trimmed cup and saucer for his demitasse, he cracked walnuts, Brazil nuts, filberts, and almonds, which we picked from their shells inside his palm, and peeled the skin from apples, oranges, and pears in single spirals, which we'd wear on our heads as crowns. This was a nightly ritual.

Sometimes I'll agree to pass my mother's praise along to Rich, while at others I'll press back. "He's half of this relationship," I tell her. "Why shouldn't he do half the cooking?"

Tonight, though, it's more satisfying to lie on our old blue couch, my damp head wetting the pillows, and start in on the slim, ugly book I find on the coffee table, a worn copy of Naipaul's *Finding the Centre*. "Hey!" Rich says, catching me, and knowing there's no book I'm more attracted to than whatever it is he's reading. "Why don't you read one of those books on your nightstand? For someone who likes things so tidy, you've got quite a pile going there." I pretend to be absorbed in the book, and for a moment the only sound is of the wooden spoon on the bottom of the skillet. "Actually, you'd really like that," he says. "It's very good."

He leaves me to my reading, but in truth I can barely keep my thoughts on the page. Maybe someday I'll learn to enjoy this as a given, but for now the fact that I'm lying on the couch while my future husband cooks makes me too excited to concentrate. Which is, of course, what I'm really saying in those calls to my mother: *All that talking paid off! I am marrying a man who makes me dinner! I am a success!*

When Rich finally calls me to the table, it's his turn to try feigning indifference, but his delight is clear. Using soy sauce and cornstarch, he has created a light sauce that holds everything together beautifully. The snap peas are bright, and the shrimp is perfectly curled and rosy: it couldn't look more professional. We stand together for a moment, admiring the look of it on the table. "We should take a picture," I offer, and he smiles proudly, though neither of us moves to get the camera. Instead, we quickly fill water glasses, scoop rice, light candles, and sit while the steam is still coming off the platter.

...

A FULL WEEK without a birthday to remember, a gift to buy, a new baby to call about, a wedding detail to solidify, or a traveling friend in town, and still the days feel hectic. So on a quiet Sunday it's nice to be alone in the kitchen, even just to set up a few cups of Jell-O, one of Rich's favorite treats. (My sisters find this as unbelievable as I first did. We know Jell-O to be a consolation dessert for dieters; that his metabolism allows him to have anything and still he chooses Jell-O leaves each of us feeling something between indignant and depressed.)

When the kettle whistles, I add a cup of boiling water and slowly stir and stir until all the granules dissolve. The steaming red liquid sends up clouds of its unabashedly artificial scent, a mix of Pixie Stix and Kool-Aid that I'm helpless against leaning into and breathing deeply. Wishing for real dessert cups on stems, I pour the Jell-O into four clear glass mugs with metal handles, add banana slices and cubes of apple, and cover each with plastic wrap. Making space for them on the top shelf of the refrigerator, there's a comfort in feeling just a little more prepared for the week ahead—the responsible squirrel, or ant, with her reserves all stocked up, versus the come-what-may grasshopper—and knowing there'll be a snack waiting for him when he goes looking. Though the moment I think this the old nagging kicks in behind it, a fear of slipping into a role I don't want; or, at any rate, running to the mental checklist.

Is it my nature, I fret lately, or my instincts? I wish I could just feel the old, straightforward feelings I used to have about the kitchen—that it was a comfort, a relief from stress, and, best of all, where my brain could unravel any problem or piece of writing I was stuck on. Now, within the context of marriage, I feel tugged between enjoying being in the kitchen and fearing that it's a trap set just for me. Though, of course, I'm constantly here, of my own volition. *Why?* I keep asking myself. If it's as simple as making him happy (as his cooking is for me: wide open, without subtext), why is there always the little devil on my other shoulder, hunting for uglier motives? Am I simply making Rich happy, or am I making him happy with me? Does my ego really require continual validation—*approval*—via Jell-O?

We've agreed that my doing the cooking and grocery shopping is temporary, so why do I continually push against it? Keeping the fruit bowl filled, unspoiled milk in the refrigerator, a ready roll of toilet paper under the vanity: there's more than a touch of June Cleaver to these, and on days when I feel that I'm too consistently the one playing this role a part of me grows frantic, wants to leave the ring on the counter and take off running, elbows pumping. A good friend of mine married a man who doesn't cook at all, and once I asked her if it bothers her that all the cooking falls to her. "Not at all," she said. "I like caring for him in that way." It's an entirely natural, sweet sentiment. So why, for me, does it start the alarms flashing? *(Danger, Will Robinson! Danger!)*

Which is hardly fair. Rich changes the tricky lightbulbs on the track lighting that I don't want to go anywhere near; replaces the water filter that I consistently let turn brown; tracks "our" investments; handles the paperwork of taxes;

will run to the market during downtime; and every few weeks takes a turn cleaning the bathroom, all while working hard for us. He's proactive about things; they're just not the things I'm proactive about. Which is where I become uncomfortable. If we were a business, though, each of us would contribute what we excelled at—each do half of the jobs, rather than alternating or splitting them down the middle. Doesn't that make sense? What makes it so frightening, then, to be the person in the kitchen making Jell-O?

Maybe it's that the jobs that fall to me—and that I'm honestly most comfortable with—are the jobs women have always done, but I imagined that I was someone who could break out of that paradigm. I thought I could avoid my mother's life, and all the tiny acts of kindness she performed and that went largely unappreciated. I love her, but I don't want to be her, in her old life.

I tried to find my voice for this in our conversations about bed-making. Rich has never been a bed-maker, but I was taught to do it as a normal part of getting ready in the morning: wake up, make bed, brush teeth, put on clothes.

"If you just turn around when you get out of it, and make it right then, you don't have to give it a second thought all day," I told him, shortly after we moved in together.

"That's not what I feel like doing when I wake up," he said.

"It takes *thirty seconds,* and then the room is immediately neater and you can think more clearly."

"I think fine when the bed's not made."

"But if you're the last one in it, it's your *job* to make it!" I insisted. Then, drawing from an inherited deck of passive-aggressive cards, "If you love me, you'll make the bed." It took all my will to resist adding the classic *I am not maid service around here!*

He shook his head in disbelief. "I'm living with a crazy dictator. You're insane."

"No, *you're* insane."

A few other intelligent remarks were exchanged, and finally we let it go. Bed-making seemed to me the quintessential easily split chore: it takes no time, there's no going out of one's way, there's no strength or particular skill involved. All it requires is a sensitivity to the fact of being a modern person in a modern marriage. Though, thinking about it again later, I realized that this wasn't true; it isn't equally demanding of us. To me, it's ingrained; it bothers me more not to do it. But to Rich, it's only something to do to please me. I get to let go of something, but he has to take something up.

Still, when I get home from work now the bed is made. Which comforts me in a way I can't fully describe. I feel that my mental stability rests on the bed's being made—an act of respect I need to see. It's a gesture that says: You are not maid service around here. You are not making the same mistakes. You are choosing well.

. . .

IF TOLD THAT I HAD ONLY ONE DAY LEFT IN THIS WORLD, I would likely spend it throwing a dinner party. I love thinking about which friends to combine. I love the balancing act of devising what to prepare and in what order and to what degree, so that everything can come together in just the right order in the end. I love setting the table and arranging the flowers (at six or even four dollars a dozen, roses are the great bargain of this bank-breaking city). And I love the morning after, when there is good bread or biscuits or a few slices of dessert waiting to be eaten with the morning coffee and the details of the night before, all hashed up to live over. (Though in the above scenario, it seems I would have to miss this part.)

I tinkered and experimented in my Los Angeles kitchen, which had more deep, splintery cabinets than my roommate Christine or I could or cared to fill, and a view of an odd clubhouse next door that belonged to a Girl Scout troop that threw loud sleepover parties and never offered us any cookies. But it was in New York that the urge to throw dinner parties entirely gripped me, and it has yet to let go.

Maybe it was the food writing I began to read, or my love-at-first-sight romance with the old Westside Market on West 110th Street, where the selection and the quality were to a degree I'd never before been offered, and so many of the jars and packages and treats that I knew from my paternal grandmother's kitchen in Brooklyn, when I was still nose-high with the counter, stocked its shelves and displays. I assumed they had all disappeared with an era, but, along with the news anchors on the local affiliates, it was all just as I'd left it.

Outside inspiration was certainly a requirement for engaging the kitchen in 9J. Though what it was, more exactly—a short refrigerator, a sink, a half-size stovetop, and fourteen inches of countertop standing shoulder to shoulder in the common room—was a "kitchenette" in real-estate terminology, a language both optimistic and coy. There was a single way to stack and arrange the pots, pans, bowls, and bakeware in the kitchenette's cabinet so that everything fit, and in the face of this storage deficit I learned to adjust in both the ways that I cooked (drying salad greens in the dish rack, using a cool oven as a sideboard) and the items I owned. The kitchenette was intolerant of anything merely decorative, or even of functional items with aspirations for display. A platter I received as a gift could only be stored wrapped in paper, on a shelf in the coat closet behind the ironing board.

The common room was a modest rectangle partly divided by the old refrigerator, which had no hole to slide back into and so stuck out three feet, blocking a person at the sink from a person on the couch. But the ceilings were high and the floors were old hardwood, and we scrubbed and waxed and painted the walls a cheerful robin's-egg blue. I had a wood dining table that I used as a desk in Los Angeles, and we dragged it to where the former occupants, whom I briefly overlapped with, had put the couch. We bought four blue IKEA dining chairs and white sheers for the windows, and Yasmine unrolled a handmade kilim from Pakistan and contributed a painting from her bedroom of two sisters in front of an ocean view, which we hung beside the table.

My sisters and I used to adore a book about a squirrel called Miss Suzy, who had a one-room house in an oak tree where she baked acorn puddings and swept her soft moss carpet with a broom of maple twigs. After 9J's transformation, I thought of it as cozily on a par with Miss Suzy's little room in the treetop. (Though this was a subjective opinion. The one time my mother visited, dropping Maria off after a Christmas visit, she'd stood quietly beside the table, still in her coat, and, finally prompted for her opinion, answered, "If I lived here, I'd feel poor." Which Maria and I had found hysterical. Tuition was twenty-seven thousand a year, and I was paying for it almost entirely with loans. "I *am* poor!" I'd told her, still laughing.)

Jean Anthelme Brillat-Savarin was a lifelong bachelor, the beloved mayor of the French town of Belley, a savorer of life's finer things, and the author of the 1825 *Physiology of Taste,* in which he so famously wrote: "Tell me what you eat, and I shall tell you what you are." In it he also coined the term *gastronomy,* defining it as "the intelligent knowledge of whatever concerns man's nourishment," and offered advice, anecdotes, and meditations on the pleasures of the table.

A tremendous host and entertainer, Brillat-Savarin found inspiration in Gasterea—the tenth muse and a girl of pure loveliness, who is happiest "where the grapevine grows, where orange trees send out their perfume, where the truffle waxes and wild game and fruits may flourish." I instead found inspiration in my grocery store and freshly scrubbed kitchenette, and I set to work planning menus and parties and throwing them with varying success.

During one of my more elaborate first attempts (stuffed clams on the half shell, which were to be nestled in a bed of coarse salt, though for three-quarters of an hour the determined mollusks refused to be parted from their shells), I cut preparation time so close to dinnertime that I left myself without an hour to shower and dress. Leaving a soup to simmer, I ran to my room, zipped myself into the dress I'd planned to look so glamorous in, pulled my hair into little more than a ponytail, and ran a lipstick over my lips as the doorbell buzzed.

My first winter in 9J, the radiator was stuck permanently on—a thing I didn't at first recognize as a problem, never having had a radiator before—and while steam spewed from the silver coils beside the table, I excitedly baked and roasted hearty winter fare. Even with the windows open, we could never coax in enough frigid night air to counterbalance the broiling oven, the ambitious radiator, and the growing number of empty wine bottles.

My friend Alex, who played football as an undergraduate, wore a sweater to one dinner, and after the first course I had to dig through my dresser for one of the extra-large T-shirts always given out at 5K races. On another occasion he brought a date, a pretty brunette we all quickly grew attached to, who made it all the way to dessert before agreeing to shed her cashmere turtleneck for short sleeves. Toward the end of too many parties that winter, flushed with heat, food, and wine, we were surely a less suave collection than we might earlier have imagined ourselves.

It took some time for me to fully surrender to the kitchenette's mandate of sparseness and efficiency. I told myself that far better cooks than I, in their modest beginnings, had learned to creatively manage in cramped or inadequate quarters; or to do far more with far less. On evenings when my triumph was particularly sweet, I liked to turn to Yasmine, or the friend drying the second load of dishes beside me at the sink, and frame the evening in exactly this way, insisting, "Someday we're going to look back and laugh and say, 'Can you believe we used to wash an entire dinner party's worth of dishes by hand!'"

It was the only way to think about both the kitchenette and my life at the time. I was moving toward an age at which student means and lifestyles were only barely palatable. The future simply *had* to hold something that would render our present situation laughable, because hand-washing a dinner party's worth of dishes, and having fifty-three dollars in savings, were only fine conditions when one imagined them as the bumpy first steps down a road to success.

M.F.K.'s kitchen in the studio above the pastry shop left even more to be desired than my own, and still I envied her that time and that place, and that kitchen. Settling into the kitchenette, my graduate-student budget, and the style of grocery shopping particular to Manhattan, I thought of her often. Of that kitchen she later wrote:

> It was perhaps five feet long, perhaps three wide, and I had to keep the door open into the other room when I stood at the burner gas-plate. There was a little tin oven,

the kind to be set on top of a stove, and a kind of box with two shelves in it, for storage instead of a table.

And there was the window, one whole wall, which opened wide and looked down into the green odorous square, and out over the twisted chimney pots to the skies of the Cote d'Or: It was a wonderful window, one of the best I can remember, and what I saw and thought and felt as I stood in it with my hands on the food for us, those months, will always be a good part of me.

My own window looked out across a few feet of courtyard to a brick wall and windows identical to my own. Nevertheless, I also felt the importance of that time in my lackluster kitchenette and believed that the thoughts and conversations I had there, and the meals I prepared in it, were a prelude to something grand. I hadn't gone back to school to become an investment banker or a lawyer but for an artist's degree. It was an enormous expense and a monumental risk—one I came to feel still more acutely as Yasmine's classmates graduated to six-figure salaries—but one that I had to believe would someday change my life for the best, while still enjoying that moment of university squalor for what it was.

. . .

THROUGH YASMINE AND Patrik we've become friends with Alessandra and Paolo, another pair of economists, who are perhaps the most considerately mannered and astonishingly nice people I've ever met. Before coming to the United States to earn their doctorates, they led entirely other, completely glamorous lives in Italy, she as a sports announcer and he as a pentathlete. (I keep waiting for my grown-up life to begin, but they are on their second rounds!) They barely nod at these other people they used to be, but the idea of them fascinates me. Do we have a single destiny, or does each decision send us toward a new fate?

While Yasmine, our social chair, is in D.C. this year, we don't want to lose touch with Alessandra and Paolo and their beautiful baby daughter, and thinking fondly of them one night it seems a nice idea to invite them to dinner. To round things out, we later think to invite Allison and James, our wedding muses, who it's easy to imagine getting along perfectly with anyone. I become so intent on reaching out to everyone and choosing a date that it's not until everything is settled that the intimidating task we've set for ourselves fully dawns on me: cooking for Italians.

"What are we *possibly* going to feed them!" I begin repeating to Rich. Alessandra is from Rome, and as a girl she used to run home from school to cook full meals for her father and brothers. And even Paolo, working out of a graduate-apartment kitchen nearly as wanting as 9J, once served us pillowy ravioli that he'd spent the day rolling out by hand. Cooking for people should be about loving them, not impressing them; but impressing is far beyond my ambitions. I feel out of my depth even offering them a meal of the general quality to which they're accustomed. And, worse, they're so polite: I could feed them risotto-turned-to-glue, and instead of teasing me they'd no doubt find something to compliment.

"Let's talk about it over dinner," Rich says, when I call from the office to bring it up again.

Maria once described a friend to me by explaining, "Normally, I think I'm a pretty good person. But when I'm with her, I feel like the world's biggest sinner." With Alessandra and Paolo, my sense of myself similarly wobbles. I have far more enthusiasm than talent in the kitchen, but around friends who rarely cook this still makes me "the friend who can cook," which buoys my confidence and delight in cooking for them. Around friends whom I think of as very good cooks, however, this logic recalibrates in the opposite direction. I feel an instant connection to our few Italian friends, recognizing in them a sensibility that's very much in line with my family's (distinctions that in high school and junior high were, of course, an embarrassment to me, as is anything that sets us apart from our peers at those ages). And still, while with some friends I feel distinctly connected to my Italian roots, around "real Italians" new hats are passed around: I become the American, and they are the Italians.

"It's the disorientation of someone out-*you-ing* you," Rich once said, nodding in recognition when I brought this up. Later, it made me think of a writing class I had with Lawrence Weschler, who used to tell us, "Set the foundation, the structure, and then you can hang as many baubles on it as you like." Maybe these wobbles of identity—and even the stakes Rich and I have been racing to set down in the still uncharted territory of our marriage, claiming dibs for our preferences— are too often about mistaking the baubles for the foundation.

Tonight we sit to a salad and a potato frittata—which I surprise us both by executing perfectly, the potatoes steamed to softness and the exterior perfectly golden in parts—determined to pin down a plan. Italian food is out of the question. I don't feel comfortable serving meat. Fish is risky, since people tend to be particular about the types they like. Chinese food is an idea, but that brings us back to fish, since the stir-frys and fried rice we make are nothing to serve to guests.

"I've got it," Rich says, pursing his lips in the cute way he does before a big reveal. "The sweet-potato stew!"

"*Nooo* . . . That was a nightmare last time, and it took forever!" But he's convinced.

"Stew is a *classic*! It's hearty—we can add more jalapeños and cilantro this time to make it really fresh and bright. . . ." He nods in confirmation to himself. "Stew is always a winner. Who doesn't like stew?"

Slowly, I come around to the idea. Keeping things intentionally casual takes some pressure off, and if I make the stew on Saturday morning I'll have enough time to clean up and let the flavors come together. "How about a double-layer chocolate cake for dessert, then?" This is my Amelia Bedelia solution. After she had "drawn" the drapes, "stolen" home plate, or baked a sponge cake of dish sponges, the naïve housemaid of my childhood library visits, when faced with a list of her trespasses, would always produce a surprise plate of perfect chocolate-chip cookies in the end, and all would be forgiven. After a dinner party when Yasmine finally scolded, "You can't apologize for every dish before it arrives at the table!" I have learned, in the face of uncertainty, always to keep an old reliable waiting in the wings.

"And that squid dish . . ." Rich says, remembering a squid and white-bean appetizer someone brought to our upstairs neighbor's potluck. "That would be good, huh?" So now he's in charge of the first course. We'll serve a watercress salad to cut the heft of the stew, a pan of corn pudding, and warm tortilla chips. A pretty bowl of clementines can go on the cleared table between the stew and the cake, and before we sit to dinner an appetizer of goat cheese with fig tapenade, which also benefits from being made in advance.

"It'll be *perfect*," Rich says. "Everyone will love it." Crisis averted, we split a slice of apple tart from the Polish bakery and retire to the couch for some television.

...

THERE IS FRESH OKRA at Pitts today, but no corn-muffin mix. Which sends me on a detour through two bodegas, grocery bags in tow, and starts me thinking about the urge that prompts a person to offer herself as hostess—my usual thought at about this point in the process. Why do some of us continually offer to take on the burden of chores and expenses, a menu to plan, a grocery list to compile, and stores to walk to one after another (the wine shop is next on my list) while heavy bags bite at our fingers? Then there is the day of chopping, baking, and preparing in advance everything that can lie waiting under foil so that one can, in the final hour, shower, dress, and emerge unflustered exactly as her guests arrive. "The half-hour before dinner has always been considered as the great ordeal through which the mistress, in giving a dinner party, will either pass with flying colours or lose many of her laurels," wrote Isabella Beeton in her 1861 *Book of Household Management,* and it's still true.

My friend Raj, an excellent cook, has a habit of serving round after round of specially prepared cocktails while, absolutely unfazed, he prepares the entire meal before his guests. By the time dinner is served, everyone is starved and smashed—a sure recipe, each time, for an appreciated meal and interesting conversation. Another friend, a French woman, calm and lovely with an apron at her waist and a cigarette aloft between two thin fingers, will prepare a delicious meal before her waiting friends, set stacks of plates and silverware on the coffee table while excusing herself to her bedroom, and then emerge stunning in a little black dress, signaling that the party can now begin.

Even Rich was the picture of calm during his first solo dinner party. A few weeks after arriving in New York, he taped together some moving boxes to create a table of sturdy squares, which we sat around on the floor. On the afternoon of the party, he bought a food processor, a stock pot, and a roasting pan, and to everyone's surprise served a beautiful carrot-ginger soup and then salmon fillets with tomatoes, anchovies, and olives over little piles of haricot vert. He insists there were a few harrowing moments during preparation, but when Yasmine and Patrik and I arrived, with Rich's younger sister, Alexandra, behind us on the stairs, he was smiling and relaxed, standing in the doorway with a chilled white wine to pour.

Despite their panache, I'm of the mind that hosting others is a trick to be pulled off, and if I haven't yet learned to feel less flustered doing it, in the past five years of trying, I have, at least, learned to look less flustered. And while I honestly derive enormous pleasure from the entire process, I still never fail to wonder *why*.

Perhaps I have been loved with carefully prepared meals for so long that it's a gesture I can't help repeating. My mother prepared our favorite dishes on our birthdays, cut the orange in my father's lunch bag so that the peel pulled off easily, wrote jokes on our lunch-box napkins, and was unfailingly a gorgeous hostess. The height of her powers was on display through the holidays. She still looks back fondly on the Christmases she gave us ("gave" is her verb, and it really is the right one—she was entirely conscious of *giving* us those moments, these memories; it was an incredible gift), and it is one of her greatest joys, I think, that all of us who were there still think back on them as well. I am among the youngest in a fleet of first cousins who still say, when we get together, "Those Christmases at your mother's were the best of our lives."

For Christmas Eve dinners, my mother would string together card tables and dining tables and host a sit-down dinner for twenty, twenty-five, thirty of us. The shopping and the preparations began weeks in advance—entire evenings were dedicated to the preparation of a single type of Italian Christmas cookie—my aunts contributed their signature dishes and desserts, and we ate course after course, taking breaks, nibbling fennel, and returning to eat. And all the while my mother was beautiful, slim, and smiling in an angora turtleneck, with her bottle-blond Farrah Fawcett hair curling at her shoulders and her makeup just so, and every dish she placed on the table was artfully arranged and delicious. She was a woman radiant in her element.

Each summer, too, my parents would take us camping (or their version of camping), and everywhere we pulled our well-equipped camper we were fed as well as if we were at home. My father is a boisterous type who collects people around him wherever he goes, and I remember well one rainy afternoon that my mother hosted a Sunday lunch for twelve (a course of pasta, then meat and vegetables, salad, and dessert with espresso). Knee to knee we sat at the camper's foldaway kitchen table, on the "living room" couch, on the folding chairs that should have been outside around the fire ring, and, needing one more seat, my sister dragged out the hamper and perched on its lid. Of this late lunch, with twelve of us waiting out the rain that pinged at the camper's roof, even my mother now says, "How did I do that?"

Maybe I continually offer myself as hostess because I have seen it done, and done well, and in the small, quiet place in my brain where I store the thoughts I barely admit to myself, I think that these are the marks of a woman's prowess, and I parade them out for anyone I suspect might appreciate such an idea: the woman who can do it all. Racing through preparations, though, I'm sometimes also struck by the irony (or is it just ridiculousness?) of having paid a gross sum to earn a degree that I thought would entitle me to a life beyond my parents', while laboring to succeed in this way in which my mother, a housewife, was perfect.

Or, if there is any *me* beyond the nature and nurture, maybe it began with my mother but has since become as much about the moment when my guests sit back from the table, sated and happy, refill their glasses, and we get to have the kind of good conversations that come only from a slow dinner with friends. Which, along with the leftover dessert in the morning, is the part I love most.

. . .

SATURDAY MORNING I'M out of bed first, and I put on a pot of water for the sweet potatoes.

"You're starting already?" Rich asks on his way to the coffeemaker.

"I want to make the stew and the tapenade now, so I can get to yoga at eleven-thirty, and then finish everything afterward." I've had a plan on paper for two days now.

"I really have a lot of work to do today," he says. "I didn't expect dinner to take over the whole day."

"It's not going to," I tell him. "It's just the beginning and end parts. I'll chop quietly."

I don't know what happened to us that Friday, but preparing the vegetables, cubing everything as evenly as possible, just for the look of it, is a pleasure today. For the tapenade, I bought a bag of dried, organic figs, and they tumble onto the cutting board still caught in the slumped positions they settled into against one another. I chop them, removing their stems, and with a few tablespoons of water let them rehydrate in a saucepan over low heat.

In Rich's family, the height of pleasure is sweet corn and cold watermelon; in mine, it's hard cherries and fresh figs. On the Sunday morning walks my sisters and I would take with our father, the route home included a stop to see our Aunt Mary and Uncle Phil, an older Italian couple, of no actual relation, whom my parents were close to. While my father sat to the pancakes Mary would have waiting (high, gorgeous pancakes; beer in the batter was her trick), my sisters and I would inspect the enormous fig tree Phil tended on their covered patio—in the winter bundling it up as carefully as a child facing the snow—though its fruit was rarely ever ripe enough for picking. Does anything require more patience than a still-green fig?

I'm careful not to burn the chopped nuts, gently toasting them in a skillet, and finally they go into a bowl with the figs, chopped capers and olives, balsamic vinegar, olive oil, chopped fresh thyme, and ground pepper. This goes into the refrigerator, and I leave the stew, uncovered, to cool on the back burner.

When I get back from the gym, Rich unplugs his computer and moves from the kitchen counter to the bed, where he works while I bake the cake, wash the salad greens, and iron the big white tablecloth—a task that, since learning to iron the sari that Yasmine bought for me to wear to her wedding, no longer seems so arduous. I'll make the corn pudding once I'm dressed, and then ice the cake while the corn pudding is in the oven.

"Are you going to make the squid soon?" I call to Rich.

"It only takes a minute. I'll do it later," he says, in a tone that translates to: I'm in the middle of a thought, don't talk to me.

All that's left, then, is the table. I bought a bouquet of rose hips on my way home from the gym, their odd starkness seeming appropriate for a cold-weather meal of stew. Wanting to keep the buds low, so we can see one another across the table, I arrange them in a white teapot that matches the dishes. When we moved into this apartment, Rich's mother gave us a full set that she insisted she didn't use anymore. I'm grateful that she's so sweet, and even more grateful that her taste is so good; there are so many pieces—more than I could have dreamed of owning—that had I not liked them there would be no avoiding them. They're bright white and modern, with two offset green parsley stems and a little decoration unique to each item: two tiny purple eggplants on the soup bowls, two carrots on the dinner plates, chilies on the salad dishes. There are even matching serving bowls, platters, salt and pepper shakers, a gravy boat, coffee cups with saucers, and the teapot with a creamer, a sugar bowl, and teacups (my favorite, with little orange kumquat halves). It gives me a jolt of pleasure to open the cabinets and see all of this stacked inside. I can now serve dessert without washing the salad plates. Such decadence!

I put out wide, shallow soup bowls, salad plates (one of which perfectly hides the red-wine stain on the tablecloth), the soft blue and red cloth napkins, silverware, water and wineglasses, and a votive on either side of the flowers. Then I wash the last few things in the sink, give the kitchen a last glance-over, and finally get into the shower.

Rich still isn't dressed. "Are you going to get ready soon?" I ask from inside my closet. "I want to wipe down the bathroom once you're out." I'm not as bad as my mother, who likes to Windex the sink, but it would be nice to get the toothpaste spittle off the mirror.

"I'll shower after I make the squid," he says, finally closing his laptop for the day. Before I turn on the hair dryer, he calls out, "Why did you set the table! Where am I supposed to prepare the squid?"

"On the counter. I cleared the cutting board for you."

"But there's all this stuff here," I hear him mutter as he takes in the cooling cakes, the clementines, the washed cilantro. I turn on the hair dryer and leave him to figure it out.

When I emerge from the closet, dressed and ready for a compliment, he's chopping the washed squid bodies into rings, and very quickly we're in each other's way. I preheat the oven and take out the big skillet that we store inside it, since it's too big for the cabinet, and have a sitcom-style moment, wheeling in one direction, then the other, looking for a place to put it.

I set up on the strip of counter beside the sink to assemble the corn pudding, but then he needs the sink again, so we momentarily swap places. Then he needs the cutting board again, so we switch back. "I'm not sure this was such a good idea," he says finally, frowning into the spice drawer.

"Don't you have a recipe?" I ask.

"No . . . I think it's pretty basic," he says, but then decides to go a new route, moving things to the table to make new room on the counter.

"You know, I did things in advance so it didn't have to be all crazy at the end, and now you're making a mess," I say. "I had everything all cleaned up."

"Chill out," he says. "If you'd left me some room, and not taken over everything, I wouldn't have to put stuff on the table."

"I left plenty of space for you."

"The dictator knows exactly how much space everyone needs."

"Will you stop calling me that!"

"Will you stop being so controlling!" he says, stabbing the last word. "And it's so hot in here now with the oven on. Will you open the window, please?"

I walk back to the bedroom and open the window, and then in silence ice the cake, slice the goat cheese into rounds, spoon the tapenade alongside it, and light the candles around the apartment while he finishes prepping, washes the dishes in the sink, and then showers and dresses. This should all be part of the fun, and it annoys me that he's ruining it. Was I really being too controlling? I've always liked things done my way. *Mom, Michelle is being bossy!* used to ring through the house, as Maria ran in from the street or the basement or the yard, or wherever I was trying to control the rules of a game. Rich huffs around now with his temper poised to lash out, thinking whatever annoyed thoughts he thinks about me, and

I run a monologue through my head of what I want to say to him, smoothing the wording, repeating it to perfection. But of course I say nothing, still the girl overly attuned to my father's temper, to any crackle in the air. The moment Rich's voice hits a certain tone something in me recoils, shuts down, and I pull back my argument before I mean to, the action as unmediated as a flinch. Neither of us says a word until the front door buzzes and we're made to act like happy normal people who have invited our friends to come and share our joy.

Both couples arrive with wine in hand and are full of compliments on the apartment, which is still a mishmash of our combined things. We throw coats on the bed and give the twenty-second grand tour to Paolo and Alessandra, who have never been here, while the baby offers herself as the perfect icebreaker through the first clumsy moments—everyone well-intentioned, but the bond still re-forming itself. Rich, too, does good work of putting everyone at ease, taking drink orders and starting conversations while I pull the corn pudding from the oven.

At the table later, the squid isn't what Rich first imagined, though it certainly could have been worse. "No, Rich, it is really, really nice," Paolo tells him with trademark earnestness. The stew is uneventful but fine, the clementines are sweet (though I should have roasted nuts to go with them), and I'm grateful for the moist chocolate cake (the handiwork of a cup of sour cream in the batter). Even the baby behaves impeccably. She sits with us at the table as though enjoying our company, neatly devours the puréed vegetables Alessandra prepared and brought with her, and then falls asleep on Paolo's shoulder.

I'm fascinated by the dynamics of both these couples.

James, a native Manhattanite, is entirely charming and un-abashedly adoring of his wife in a way that makes Rich have to nudge me to stop from staring; my mother would defi-nitely think him an ideal husband. Alessandra and Paolo, by contrast, are steady pillars side by side. Never mind finger-prints and snowflakes—how much more interesting is it that each couple has a unique power structure, their own dy-namic? "You never know what goes on in people's houses," my mother likes to say, which, of course, is true. The delicate mechanisms of a relationship are a balance of wheels and gears and hands visible only to the two inside it.

While we're finishing dessert, Allison plucks a rose hip from the teapot bouquet. "I think these are edible," she tells me, while the others dissect a soccer match.

"Yeah, in some form . . ." I agree, definitely not wanting her to eat it. "But maybe something has to happen to it first?"

She brings it closer to her mouth, with her gaze on me. I remember an essay James wrote during a workshop we had together, in which he described meeting Allison and thinking she was like a Serengeti cat, ready to pounce. Which is ex-actly right. She has an assured strength about her that's mes-merizing, and blue-gray eyes that seem to grasp whatever she settles them on. About a month before Rich proposed, I con-fided to her that I was upset he hadn't done it yet, and the next time she saw him she pulled him aside.

"She told me to shit or get off the pot," Rich told me later, wholly admiring of her bluntness.

"James," I say, trying for a joking tone. "Your wife is eating my centerpiece."

He looks at her, amused, and with her gaze still on me she frowns a little and sets the rose hip on the table.

The conversations move easily, and each time the baby wakes, refreshed from her cat nap and delighted by the candlelight, she charms us all. James also had a colorful life before graduate school, interning for the Maysles brothers. Toward the end of the night, he tells a story about running around the Lower East Side at 2 A.M., trying to buy enough pint-size containers of cream to fill a bathtub, after someone on a film set once had a last-minute idea for a sexy scene. By the time he returned, with five shopping bags of heavy cream, they'd decided to do something else with the girl.

While he's talking, Rich takes my hand and squeezes it. "Sorry," I say softly, telling myself that I will be a more relaxed, chilled-out person.

"Sorry," he whispers back, and puts a kiss in my palm.

"So what happened to all the cream?" Paolo asks.

"The shoot finished at 5 A.M., and on my way home I left it against the gate of a coffee shop," James says, pouring more wine. "I really hope they used it."

MARIA'S I-DON'T-BAKE DOUBLE-LAYER CHOCOLATE CAKE

FOR THE CAKE:

> 1 box devil's food cake, with chocolate pudding
> in the batter; or, short of that, add a box
> of instant chocolate pudding to the cake
> mix
> 1 cup whole-fat sour cream

¾ *cup water*
½ *cup oil*
3 large eggs
1 *teaspoon vanilla extract*

FOR THE FROSTING:

1 *stick butter, melted*
⅔ *cup unsweetened cocoa powder*
3 cups confectioners' sugar, sifted
⅓ *cup sour cream*
1 *teaspoon vanilla extract*

PREHEAT THE OVEN TO 350 DEGREES. In a medium-size bowl, combine all the cake ingredients and mix them well with a hand beater or spatula. Then pour the batter into two 9-inch greased cake pans and bake for 28 to 32 minutes, or until exactly the moment a toothpick comes out clean and the cakes have slightly pulled away from the sides of the pan. (I really think not baking it for even a minute more than it needs is the secret to super-moistness. Along with, of course, all that delicious sour cream.)

The frosting recipe above is just as Maria gave it to me. But I like a lighter frosting, and not quite so much of it, so I cut the recipe in half, add an extra tablespoon or two of sour cream, and then frost only the tops of both cakes, which is still very pretty when you stack them. I've also made this with Ghirardelli's Premium Baking Cocoa, which is sweetened and results in a frosting as sweet as most; whereas the unsweetened cocoa makes a more reserved, grown-up-style icing. Either way, it's very simple.

Mix the butter and cocoa until smooth. Add the confectioners' sugar and sour cream a little at a time, alternating between the two and blending on low speed. Add the vanilla last, and beat for one minute.

The frosted cake can sit for a day on a covered cake stand at room temperature (in a cool place, far from the stove is ideal), but I'd store any leftovers in the refrigerator; if you add a little extra sour cream to the icing, as I do, this hardly stiffens the texture.

CORN PUDDING

THIS RECIPE LIKELY came from the spine of a box of corn-muffin mix, though it was given to me by a girl who sublet my roommate's bedroom one summer. She and her boyfriend left stains on the couch cushions and scuffed the kitchen walls where a nicer apartment would have had a chair rail. But this recipe is so brainlessly easy, and so delicious warm or cold, that after I made it a few times I considered us squared up. She was actually a very nice girl.

2 eggs
1 16-ounce can corn, drained
1 16-ounce can creamed corn

½ stick butter, melted
1 box cheap corn-muffin mix

PREHEAT THE OVEN TO 350 DEGREES. In a
medium-size bowl, beat the eggs and then add the
corn, creamed corn, melted butter, and muffin mix
(which is to say, put an ingredient or two between
the melted butter and the eggs, so they don't start to
cook). Stir until *just* combined. Bake for 20 to 25 minutes until the top is golden and an inserted toothpick
comes out clean.

NOTE:

What is in that fifty-nine-cent box of muffin mix,
anyway? Cheap cornmeal, sweeteners, and a leaven-
ing agent? While it would partially defeat the point of
how simple this recipe is, a more clever person might
benefit from figuring out how to replace the muffin
mix with a good, coarsely ground cornmeal, sugar,
baking soda or powder, and some salt.

". . .

"I REALLY *ENJOYED* YOU GIRLS," MY MOTHER LIKES TO SAY, particularly after witnessing a stranger suffer the antics of a naughty child—a thing that wouldn't have been tolerated on the tight ship she ran. She was strict, but we listened, and she knew how to make things fun. She can turn a meal's smallest anomaly—an unusual utensil, an extra preparatory step— into a production everyone clamors for a role in. Suddenly it's fun to layer the table with newspapers for steamed crabs, or push the saved Popsicle sticks into apples to prepare them for caramel. On the annual night that *The Wizard of Oz* or *The Sound of Music* came on TV, she would make popcorn in her biggest double-handled pot and let us drag a slumber party's worth of pillows and blankets to the living room, making a special occasion out of really nothing at all.

Actual holidays, then, can hardly be overdone. Each year around August, my mother begins announcing dibs on Christmas Eve. My sisters and I know that it's her favorite holiday to host, but she doesn't take any chances and begins securing the guests around her table early. There is a menu to plan and refine, table linens to iron, the second refrigerator to plug in and freeze up, and out come the extra dining-table leaves with their custom-cut protective pads, so lasting and of another era that they almost speak of a trousseau. (Later, once the holiday is over and the last platter and champagne glass have been carefully put away, the table will be reduced again and for days seem too small, finally prompting some-one to ask, "Did we take out too many leaves?" But no, our eyes just grew used to the spectacle.)

Rich's parents are more modest in their celebrations. Having their children's faces gathered around the table, the family re-assembled, is delight enough for them. His mother prepares a beautiful meal—a turkey, stuffing, cranberry sauce, green beans, and sweet potatoes on Thanksgiving; a lamb roast with mint jelly for Christmas—and the family happily eats together. "It's just going to be us?" I asked Rich the first time I went home with him for Thanksgiving, not grasping the concept.

I like a holiday to feel *big;* he thinks it's cozier small. He wonders if maybe my family doesn't go a little overboard, isn't a bit ridiculous about these things, and I wonder if his is too ca-sually letting life pass them by, not seizing the day; though these conversations, which become less about him and me than about the Chinese vs. the Italians, tend not to go very far.

I suspect Rich also prefers his holidays small because they require less commitment. Celebrating *big* means giving one-self over to a day of dressing up, going to church, rounds of kisses hello, and then hours of talking and eating. While when celebrating small, any comfortable clothes will do, and a person so inclined can work right up until the moment he's called to the table.

We work a lot. Surely I work harder now as a result of knowing Rich. He has a drive that's contagious, and over the years I've watched people close to him take up the same hobbies, learn the same languages, even travel to the same places, so infectious are even his interests. I started writing stories in grade school, but it wasn't until I met Rich that I found the confidence to think I might try it as a profession.

He's also very much his father's son. Because his father's work is not a thing to retire from but who he is, when we visit he's either in his office or taking a break—the sense being that everything that's not work is a break from work, which is a sentiment that has carried over to our home as well. *You become one parent and marry the other.*

New York itself is nearly fuel enough. "This city is the best of the best!" the magazine's publisher likes to say, and it's difficult not to feel already left behind, an urgency to keep a shoulder dug in and pressing forward or be swept under the machinery. Rich and I spend a good portion of most weekends writing, or feeling guilty that we should be. When an entire sunny Saturday in our windowless living room becomes too much for me, I try to coax him out for a walk, a game of tennis. Sometimes he concedes, but more often he tells me quietly, "If I'm going to succeed at this, these are the years I need to make it happen."

In Rich's old Upper West Side apartment, a songwriter lived overhead, and hearing him upstairs at his piano—like living with Roger Radcliffe, minus the Dalmatians—was the perfect motivation to keep us planted at our laptops. In Williamsburg, we step outside to see who has been busy during the night. To the frustration of Mayor Bloomberg's Anti-Graffiti Task Force, which twice now has scrubbed our building's brick exterior with a chemical slurry that sends us running to close the windows, the neighborhood is a canvas for artists of every stripe. A few blocks away, the elusive Swoon, a woman of about our age who keeps her real name a secret, has pasted up a new cutout: a portrait of a somber woman, in which the ornate razor cuts pulling her from the paper (as much as Michelangelo unburied the sculpture waiting inside each block of marble) are fine as pencil lines. On the next block is a two-part stencil. Is it a Banksy?—the British artist whose smart, satirical pieces awe and frustrate police and museum staffs, flummoxed between tearing them down and selling to the highest bidder? A stenciled black-and-white girl in pigtails jumps rope with the end of a chartreuse-painted wire. It wriggles twenty feet down the sidewalk and up a wall to a stenciled circuit breaker and a black-and-white boy, who stretches on tiptoe to flip the switch. Find these in a gallery and you'll pay five to six figures; get caught putting them up and you get a night in jail. ("They give you milk and bologna sandwiches," a friend tells us from experience.) Everyone is working. Everyone is pushing.

As tempting as it is to spend a Saturday relaxing in the park, or grilling on the roof with friends, not answering the creative urge leaves a person feeling hollow. When Rich's sweet temperament turns cranky, I know it's been too many days since he last opened the Word file for his novel in progress. These days, he works late into the night on assignments to pay for the wedding, rather than on ideas that compel him. Even the more successful artists we know accept commissions they don't want, or take on corporate projects to pay the bills. Too few people can support themselves with the work they put their hearts into.

"You should always come first to your husband's work," my mother used to tell me. But the balance is harder still—if one is even possible—when it's two people with careers and, worse, creative ambitions. My thoughts return again and again to the Viktor Frankl quote pinned above my desk: "What is to give light must endure burning."

...

EASTER COMES EARLY this year, and by mid-March my family has been discussing it for weeks—what to eat, what time, who will come. All that's been settled is that my mother will host. Rich has several deadlines looming, plus a business trip the Monday after. We don't have the time, or a reserved rental car, to visit his parents in Boston, but he's reluctant to commit even to an afternoon in New Jersey with my family. I find it stressful to leave decisions open-ended; I like to have a plan and let it structure the day, week, month. But to Rich a set plan is more stressful, distracting him from all that comes before it. Holidays, then, emphasize our differences and escalate our stresses, especially when there are other people involved, gifts to buy, or travel arrangements to make.

We've done an awkward dance through this week, with me wanting an answer but not wanting to nag, and him wanting to avoid the distraction while feeling the pressure of my waiting for his answer. "So are you two coming?" Bridget asks during our morning phone calls, once we've discussed where I can get a blow-dry on the morning of the wedding, or the marriage license that I need to apply for in her county. The Wednesday before Easter, Rich and I finally talk before I leave the office and agree that I will visit my mother and help

Bridget and Wes with some pre-wedding house projects, and he will stay behind to work.

Walking to the subway afterward, I think about it again and realize that as a girlfriend I would have insisted that he stop working for a holiday, and as a boyfriend he would have conceded and come with me. Maria is as careful in her dating as I was, if not more so, and I hear myself telling her: If you're too rigid, things break; there's a difference between compromising integrity and being flexible. Which she insists she knows, though to me it's not always clear which I'm doing. Tonight, though, I decide the bending is okay. I feel less driven these days to impress my family and present them with a boyfriend who can put on good clothes, respect our traditions, and behave at the Sunday table, and more concerned about showing Rich that we're two hardworking members of the same team. Maybe this is what marriage is: a shifting of loyalties.

Still, not getting my way on something so big might ordinarily justify a bit of brooding on my part, but when I unlock the front door, Rich is standing at the counter with dinner preparations under way, and my mood is quickly lifted. We invited the upstairs neighbor for dinner tonight, and Rich shopped this afternoon and made a brilliant discovery: a vacuum-sealed packet of faux ground beef. Moist and dark brown, it's a complete evolution from the boxes of yellow veggie burger powder that Maria and I mixed with water and formed into patties in high school.

Rich warms the taco shells on a cookie sheet in the oven and works two skillets over medium flames on the front burners, one of free-range, organic beef—which is intensely soft, a beautiful Valentine's red, and interestingly loath to crumble—and the other of the new faux beef, which the

neighbor and I both mistake for the real thing. Which is incredible—such *texture*! we enthuse; how do they make it look
so *real*?—though also a little horrifying. The free-range, organic beef is such a far cry from what we know ground beef
to look like that it begs the question of what exactly it was we
all grew up eating.

But tacos, so brilliant! How did we not think of this
sooner? Rich sets out a platter of iceberg lettuce, chopped red
tomatoes, black olives, and shredded Cheddar; I cut limes for
the beers; and the three of us clink bottles and dig in. The
faux beef is spicy, the sour cream cold and tangy, and an un-
familiar brand of salsa from the Mexican bodega surprisingly
fragrant. Suddenly "ground beef" is back in my life and my
mind is off and racing: meatballs, meat loaf, meat sauce,
sloppy joes, shepherd's pie. What other new options does this
usher in?

...

AFTER WORK ON FRIDAY, I catch a train out of Penn Station. Always I take the window seat, liking the view of back-
yards for town after town. If the fronts of houses are the
neatly groomed selves we show off to neighbors, then back-
yards are our early-morning selves, disheveled, more honest.
When the houses give way to woods, nearing the western
edge of New Jersey, I count how many deer I can spot before
the light fades entirely. Today, five: three fawns and two does.

Rich calls just as the train slows into the final station to
check that I've arrived safely, and before we hang up he asks,
"Are they going to judge me for not coming?" Probably, I
think.

"We'll see," I tell him. Not dropping everything for a holiday is uncharted terrain. Poor Wes. He's been waiting a decade for me or Maria to give him a brother-in-law, some male reinforcement at the table, and when I finally do he's managed to get out of a holiday.

My mother's house is a few miles from Wes and Bridget's, and early on Saturday we pick up my nephew and two nieces to make bread dolls, an Easter tradition since, at least twenty years ago, an older cousin gave us a Tomie dePaola book about an Italian American boy who brings his American friend to visit his very Italian grandmother. Cultural misunderstandings ensue, but in the end she charms them both with her bread dolls, which involve braiding a cinnamon-laced dough around a hard-boiled egg—essentially making it the pale face of a tightly swaddled newborn. The recipe is on the last page of the book, heavily stained from years of use. While we're wrapping the dough to put it somewhere warm, Maria and her best friend since the third grade, who also now lives in Los Angeles, call for the recipe. None of us is ready to give up the tradition.

While the dough is rising, we decorate the eggs. Gone are the wobbly wire lassos that came with the dye kits we used to make yellow and blue turn green; markers and blobby ink pens rule the day now. "Won't these leach into the eggs? Aren't they dangerous?" I press my mother, inspecting them skeptically.

"They never eat the eggs anyway," she says. "Leave them alone—they're having fun." And they are. Each of them—the eldest, already a leggy blonde at eleven; my nephew, now ten, long-lashed and handsomer by the day; and the six-year-old, who, though without my curls, looks just like me at that age—is furrowing a brow or biting a lip, in deep concentration over their eggs.

"Are you excited about the wedding?" I ask them while we each braid our portion of dough around our eggs; one long rope of dough goes over and around the top of the egg, and a second rope, half the length, gets pinched at its center, behind the "newborn's" head. My nephew will be the ring bearer, my younger niece the flower girl, and the older one a bridesmaid. For Bridget's 1990 wedding, she chose fuchsia bridesmaids' dresses with pearl headpieces that dipped with a teardrop bead above the eyes; in her wedding video, braces flashing, I was already threatening payback. She has lucked out on that front.

To my nieces, "just wear something that makes you feel beautiful" has translated to puffy white wedding-style dresses of their own. When the bread dolls are baked and my mother drops us all back at my sister's, the girls race me to their closets to show off dresses, jewelry, shoes, all of them white and sparkly.

"Okay, Aunt Shell Shell," Bridget announces, arriving at the closet door with her to-do list for the house. "Party's over."

It's hard to believe this is the same house they drove me out to last Easter, a week after the closing. It was dark and filthy, and we'd held our scarves over our faces to keep from gagging in a bedroom that had been treated as a giant litter box. They've worked miracles since then, scraping, spackling, repainting each of the kids' bedrooms, and replacing long stretches of drywall. Wes sanded the floors in each of the kids' rooms down to the bare wood and varnished from scratch. Even the hallway has fresh paint and new flooring. They're still laughing about a night Bridget woke and found that Wes wasn't in bed. It was 3 A.M., all the lights were on, and she discovered him passed out on the plastic-covered floor of what was to be my younger niece's bedroom, paintbrush still in hand.

There's a sign on the door to the main bathroom, which the wedding guests will use, telling the kids to keep out. No toilet, no sink, no tub, no drywall. Everything has been ripped out, and Wes is waiting for his father to help him with some plumbing. I'm not sure which of us this worries more.

Disgustingly, the cats left their marks in several rooms, well down to the wood beneath the varnish. With the help of a few brawny neighbors, Wes's agenda today is to sand the floors of the attached living and dining rooms with a rented drum sander. It stands in the corner now, looking like a filthy descendant of the old floor polishers that men used to guide over linoleum in the Woolworth's and school hallways of my childhood, the shrill, spinning, polishing brush making the machines seem to hover weightlessly.

These two rooms together are a wide-open space, with floor-to-ceiling windows on two sides. The walls, previously dark green, have been sanded and primed white, and even without light fixtures the room glows with sunlight, warm and inviting. If May 14 calls for hurricane rains, my plan is to move the rented tables in here. (Bridget has promised not to furnish these rooms until the wedding is over.)

The men crack open beers and discuss strategy. The prints of their sneakers and work boots crisscross and loop in the sawdust on the floor, like the dotted lines that follow the kids in *Family Circus* cartoons. Wes offers me a beer, but I decline.

As nice as this whole alcohol-and-power-tools thing is, if someone loses a finger, he's not pinning that on me.

My job today is to help Bridget transfer to the basement a gigantic fish tank the previous owners left behind. Then we're going to shampoo the damp basement's squishy aqua carpet until it's clean enough that she feels comfortable finally bringing down the piles of boxes and odds and ends that, with the fish tank, have been crowding the family room.

If I were to move, I would also leave this tank behind. It's three hundred gallons and filled with mean-looking black fish, nearly the shape and size of Ping-Pong paddles. Bridget and I stare at them for a little while, making the same disgusted face.

"I think these fish are actually kind of expensive," she says. "I saw something that looked like them in the pet store once, but smaller, and those were fifty bucks each."

Really? We count eight of them, and discuss whether the fish store would buy them from us instead, or if you can sell fish on eBay.

Offering a Plan C, she says hopefully, "Maybe we should just throw the fish in the pond and then put the tank at the end of the driveway. I think these tanks are also kind of expensive."

"Actually, if we put these fish in the pond they'd probably wind up eating all the other fish, and ravaging the pond's ecosystem, and eventually pulling in the geese and squirrels and small fawns drinking at the water's edge," I tell her. "And then one night you'd be getting ready for bed, walking through the house turning off the lights, and you'd look up and see their big silver eyes blinking in the window."

She frowns at me.

Plan A it is. She scoops the flopping fish into two thoroughly rinsed mop buckets, where they line themselves up like dark slashes. Then, with plastic Super Bowl cups we can throw away afterward, we start scooping water into a big spackle bucket, which we take turns emptying outside. It's slow work, made worse by the stench stirred up by the fish, which, in their resistance to being carried away, have unsettled a disgusting amount of fish poo that settled below the rocks. We try not to breathe, and keep our faces as far as possible from any splashes. After twenty minutes or so of this, my smallest niece, rifling in the storage space beneath the tank, holds up some tubing and asks, "What's this?"

It's an apparatus that attaches to the filter motor and sucks out the water to do exactly what we're doing. Such luck! The child is congratulated on her brilliance. There's even an old instruction sheet, which Bridget follows. We plug the filter back in, she connects her end to it, I hold my end over the bucket, and then, cautiously, she flips the switch. A little water dribbles into the bucket.

"I feel like we're giving the tank a colonic," she says, and we laugh the same *glug-glug-glug* Maisto laugh, which then makes us laugh harder. A little collection of rocks rattles through the filter and quickly swooshes out the tube with a rush of stinky brown water that snakes the tube from my hand. It sprays the two of us, the wall, the floor, the edge of her black leather sofa. I might have caught the tube sooner had I not instinctively clamped my mouth and eyes shut.

The tube finally back in the bucket, Bridget stands with the shocked expression of someone who has had paint thrown at her, and my little niece, who somehow avoided the spray, goes from squealing to delightedly pointing and shouting, "*Ewww!*" My shirt is sprinkled with little brown bits.

Wes comes in from the living room, followed by the neighbors, and couldn't be more pleased by our situation. I wipe a dry portion of one sleeve across my mouth, my lips still pursed. Wes is covered with dust, holding a beer, and swallowing a laugh in order to deliver his punch line. "You want that drink now?" he says, grinning.

. . .

EASTER SERVICE IS early at the church where the wedding will be, because the pastor gives a second sermon at a larger church at the more expected hour. It's a tiny church, narrow and white, with a classic steeple and a red front door. On both sides it's flanked by a modest cemetery with weathered head-stones dating to the eighteenth century. It looks more like a quaint thing to drive by than a functioning church, but it's just a mile from Bridget's house, down a skinny street of big oaks—an unexpected find in this rural, wide-open country.

Standing in my office doorway recently, Kay asked what kind of church it is. Rich and I had driven out the night before for our pre-wedding meeting with Pastor Ross, a lively white-haired woman near retirement age. During our long talk, I couldn't at all guess what she thought of us, particularly when Rich went into a long explanation—after she'd asked how we are at communicating—about how I go silent when I'm upset with him, but I'll still say "Bless you" when he sneezes. Before we stood to leave, though, she surprised me by saying, "I think Rich is *awesome!*" My first thought had been, *Can you tell that to my mother?*

"Um, Unitarian?"

"Oh, really? Aren't they the far-out, super-accepting ones?" This is the sort of thing she approves of.

"Are they? No, wait . . . Maybe it's *United Methodist*."

"You aren't sure," she laughed. "I thought the church thing was important to you."

"It is . . . I'm just not so hung up on the denominations. As long as they believe in Jesus, it's all good." She nodded in a way that called me out on a small lack of integrity.

"It's also *really, really* convenient. . . ."

Today Pastor Ross reads the traditional Easter text, focusing on the difficulty of belief, and drawing out the idea that Mary Magdalene, arriving at the tomb, was shocked to find Jesus missing. He'd been a broken record, repeating again and again his plans to rise on the third day, but even the people who believed in him and loved him most were slow to grasp that he had actually done this.

I believe, I really do. And I understand how my mother can be confused and upset that I'm willing to marry someone who doesn't entirely share my thinking—and I feel so *guilty* about this! If I were really a good Christian, shouldn't this be unimaginable? I worry about Rich, and for his soul, and I pray for him. I ask God to fill his heart with His love, and to create in it a yearning for Him. And maybe if I were a stronger person I would leave Rich and continue to pray for him, and go and be with someone else who would encourage me on my spiritual path. But would that even *count* if it wasn't what I honestly wanted? Wouldn't it just be a sort of physical lip service if I did something because in my head I thought it was the right thing to do but in my heart I didn't want it?

The Christian argument is that I'm supposed to do it anyway; that Christ demands sacrifice. "But isn't it better to be with Rich, leading by example?" I once told my mother weakly, trying to wriggle out of this argument. "After all, Jesus sat to eat with the sinners, who needed him, not with the holy men."

When we finally bow our heads, I pray: *Thank you, Lord, for dying for me. Please don't hate me for marrying Rich. Please don't let this marriage fail.*

After the service I approach Pastor Ross to say hello and she smiles at me warmly. "Where's Rich?" she asks.

"I'm afraid he had a lot of work to take care of at home and couldn't make it," I tell her.

"That's too bad. Please wish him a happy Easter for me," she says, her affection genuine.

Like Rich, my mother was not at church on this holiest day of the Christian calendar. She was too busy preparing for company. ("I watched it on TV this morning while I stuffed the clams!" she insists when we call her out on it.) She has also filled dozens of plastic eggs with chocolate, candy, change, and cheap baubles, so the kids can have a hunt, and, hurrying around the kitchen now—putting on music, lighting candles—she sends Bridget and me outside to hide the eggs, an annoying task that sends our heels sinking into the damp, grassless winter lawn.

My Aunt Teresa (whom all the cousins call Tee Tee) arrives from Long Island with the excellent mozzarella and semolina bread from the delicatessen near her house. "Where's Rich?" she asks. Working, I tell her; he's got a lot of deadlines this week. An older cousin arrives from Pennsylvania with her husband and four children. "Where's Rich?" they ask. He's traveling this week, so he has a lot of deadlines, I explain. With each new guest, I feel more compelled to defend him.

Inside, my mother has the kitchen table covered with a sampling of her classic appetizers. "We're only fifteen today," she tells me quietly, explaining what she thinks is a minimal spread. There are two long strombolis shining under an egg glaze (one with meat, one without); two dozen stuffed clams on the half shell (fake plastic shells she'll later scrub and pack away); golden phyllo-dough triangles filled with sweetened ricotta; a platter of raw vegetables and cheeses; and a dish with white slices of the milky mozzarella. Still, she's happy for the bustling house, and she works and talks and orchestrates. She has Bridget pouring drinks, Wes carefully lifting a heavy ham from the bottom rack of the oven, and Tee Tee tossing her famous salad. Her secret, my aunt tells one of the children, offering a stiff romaine leaf, is "salt, pepper, and lots of tasting." In goes another shake of salt.

We sit around the kitchen table, eating and catching up, and once we slow down and are feeling full my mother announces that dinner is ready. How we arrange ourselves is also a matter under her direction, and she instructs us to find our names around the table, on the place cards she has hurriedly made herself—a task that, once upon a time, Maria and I would have thrown ourselves into with a sleeve of colored markers.

In the kitchen, my mother ladles while Tee Tee serves the orecchiette she also brought, along with her homemade marinara. She's a big advocate of advance planning and freezing. Once, Rich and I listened to the two of them debate the best way to cook and freeze broccoli rabe. After what might have been twenty minutes, Rich leaned over and whispered: "I feel like I'm in a Nora Ephron movie."

After the pasta our bowls are cleared, but we hold on to our forks; I'm told to sit back down, and my sister and aunt bring out the next course: the ham Bridget glazed, a zucchini Parmigiana, made on my account, sautéed string beans, stuffing, an artichoke pie, sweet potatoes, and, of course, the salad, which my aunt will make sure is eaten down to its last leaf.

My mother is finally seated and relaxed, or as relaxed as a hostess can be; but there's something unsettled in her face. There are bodies; gathered around her table, but it's still not what it used to be: folding tables attached to card tables attached to dining tables, with two or three of her four sisters and their families, or one or two of her five brothers and their families, and all the little cousins with matching curls and smiling eyes, strongly bearing the DeFonte genes. Is this where her thoughts go?

My grandfather owned a delicatessen, which my cousins still run today, on the Brooklyn waterfront, south of Williamsburg. My aunts still rub their wrists, remembering the Saturdays they spent down at "the store," as they still call it, wrapping thousands of sandwiches for the football weddings that were popular during leaner times in Brooklyn. Entering a rented hall with communal tables, guests would say what kind of hero they wanted and catch it as it spiraled toward them. In a kitchen together, my mother and her sisters are still this well-organized staff, talking and catching up but with their eyes on the squid being stuffed, the sauce being stirred, the salad salted.

Is this what she thinks back to, the laughing they did, the fun they had with their growing broods and my grandmother still alive, who would sit in the center of a chaotic kitchen and finally beat back the noise by breaking into a warbling aria? My parents were a poor fit from the start, but they worked at that marriage for twenty-three years. Now, even that time has passed. Everyone is grown, moved away. All the little nieces and nephews have children of their own—and even some of them have children. And still, my mother can't help but dig in her heels, wanting to hold some part of it in place. We tell her that Bridget wants to host, that it's the next generation's turn. "I'm getting older now; soon it'll be your turn," she says. Though with each new holiday she insists that time hasn't come yet.

The kids head back down to the basement for a second round of running and screaming while the table is cleared, the dishwasher filled, pots and pans scrubbed, tea and espresso brewed, and the boxed desserts plated. Over the rush of the faucet and the clattering plates, I hear my mother instructing my cousin on how to fill the cream puffs she's made, cutting them three-quarters of the way so that they're a cap on a hinge. I find it more appetizing to have just one or two carefully made desserts, but my mother likes a full table; the excess, to her, is more festive. In the dining room, Bridget and I refold the cloth napkins, brush crumbs into our cupped hands, set out dessert plates and forks, tea cups and espresso cups, milk and sugar pots, and straighten and push in the chairs, making the table seem inviting again. Finally, someone shouts down the stairs that dessert is on the table, and the kids rush back up, flush-faced and disheveled—and much needed. Since only people ten years and younger can fathom chocolate mousse after the meal we've eaten.

Tee Tee insists that it's no trouble to drop me off on her way to Long Island, though I know this will send her through an extra borough and add thirty minutes to her ride. But she's happy to do it, and I like spending the time with her. She was a child psychologist and, like my mother and their mother, has always known how to have fun with kids, creating silly songs, taking us on trips, devising games to distract us as we stood in long lines. Now I appreciate her conversation; she's measured in her thinking and likes to consider perspectives, debate. Through the years, ever the therapist, she would ask me interested but provocative questions about Rich: Why do you love him? What would you say are his best and worst qualities? After my engagement, my mother had her worried as well, but we've since discussed it and she respects my decision.

Tonight we talk for a while and eventually settle into a comfortable silence, inching with hundreds of taillights toward the Outerbridge. Last Sunday, making dinner with Rich, I suggested turning on some music, but he paused. "Let's enjoy the silence a little longer," he suggested. "Embrace the somberness of Sunday night. . . ." There was no time for my usual Sunday blues today, but, sitting in the dark now, my mind races to the week ahead. At work, I have meetings each day and a feature story to finish.

Lately I've been missing the Sundays I knew as a girl: waking to the smell of simmering sauce, a big late lunch after church, and then, close to bedtime, a light snack. Relatives came to us or we went to them, but either way there was a slow afternoon at the table and leftover desserts the next morning. My father read *The New York Times,* went for a walk with his pipe, took a nap, relaxed.

Now, I rush through each day, feel whole weeks slip past me. I want to be "in the moment," as the lithe yoga instructor at the gym tells us, her class of New Yorkers all struggling to relax. "I hold my stress in my butt," a substitute instructor said one Saturday. "Think about where you hold your stress and relax it." My mouth. Lately, I catch myself sitting at my desk with my lips clenched like the clasp of an old-lady coin purse. When did I start doing this?

It's impossible not to envy the Italians their talent for living. On a vacation once, Rich and I took a train to a pretty town outside Milan and arrived during siesta. Outside the station, hundreds of unlocked bicycles waited under the high sun for their trusting owners to return. While they slept, we walked hot narrow streets, lit candles in empty churches, and disturbed only a gray cat, reclining in the shadows of a courtyard. What does it take to be able to say *basta*—enough—and allow yourself the kindness of resting through the most unforgiving hours of an afternoon?

It's clear to me that this is what life is about. Rich feels it too, I know, but I suspect I'm more inclined to surrender to such a low-key existence. When we travel, he's curious, enthusiastic, embraces everything. When it's time to go, though, he seems refreshed and ready to rejoin the race, while I find myself still wondering, *Who would I be if that were my tiny cottage on the hilltop?* But now's not the time. Now is the time to push. And, in fairness, even a few Italians have felt the same. In *The Writing Life,* Annie Dillard tells the story: "After Michelangelo died, someone found in his studio a piece of paper on which he had written a note to his apprentice, in the handwriting of his old age: 'Draw, Antonio, draw, Antonio, draw and do not waste time.'" The clock ticks for us all.

Tee Tee leaves me at my door with a hug and an extra kiss for Rich, after I assure her that I can handle my small suitcase and the shopping bag of leftovers my mother insisted on packing for him. Inside, he's sitting at his computer with papers spread around him, and a take-out container from the Thai place he hates. Take-out options on Easter must be slim.

"How was it?" he asks, getting up to relieve me of my suitcase.

"Good," I tell him. "You were the most popular person there."

ARTICHOKE PIE

> *1 small onion, chopped*
> *3 tablespoons olive oil*
> *1 box frozen artichoke hearts, defrosted*
>   *enough that you can split them*
>   *length-wise*
> *Water*
> *Salt and pepper to taste*
> *Fresh or dried parsley*
> *3 eggs*

> Grated cheese (Parmesan or a Pecorino-
>   Romano blend)
> Bread crumbs (Italian style, panko, or a mix
>   of the two)
> ¼ cup vegetable oil

SET THE OVEN TO 350 DEGREES. In a saucepan, sauté the onions in the olive oil over medium heat. Before the onions color, add the artichokes, a few tablespoons of water, salt and pepper, and the parsley to taste. Stir this gently, allowing the artichokes to break up, for 5 to 10 minutes, or until everything is well warmed through. When it tastes like something you could eat as is, pour it into an 11 x 7-inch baking dish or a glass pie pan (it's nice to be able to see the two layers before you serve it).

In a medium-size bowl, beat the eggs, then add to them: 2 handfuls (heaping palmfuls) of grated cheese, 4 handfuls of bread crumbs, the vegetable oil, and ¼ cup of water at a time, until the consistency is like a thick muffin batter. (You'll likely need between ¼ cup and ½ cup of water, plus a smidge, depending on how big your handfuls are. If it feels too watery or loose, add a little more bread crumbs and cheese.) Pour this over the artichokes and onion, spread it evenly, and then bake for 45 minutes, or until the stuffing top is golden and begins to pull away from the sides of the pan.

CREAM PUFFS

WHAT THESE ARE, really, is profiterole. But my mother has always called them cream puffs, and if you have done her a favor, or invited her over, or in some way deserve a pat on the back, you can expect a big plate of them filled with a creamy vanilla pudding and dusted with powdered sugar. It's worked out well for me to follow her lead and make these on any occasion when a dessert or a tender gesture is welcome or required.

I once bought a skirt in Chinatown for fifteen dollars, which is what I told my friend Yasmine when she complimented it. "Don't say that to anyone else!" she insisted. "The next time someone compliments it just say, 'Thank you!' And, if you must, tell them you bought it *downtown*." Which, technically, was correct. Likewise, when first-timers bite into these cream puffs they will suddenly view you through new eyes. They will rave and compliment you, and silently become slightly jealous, assuming that you have a handle on certain culinary techniques they regrettably do not. In that moment, you must decide to brush away the aura of mystique newly enfolding you and explain that this dessert takes ten minutes and five ingredients, and two monkeys could make it. Or you can smile demurely and just say, "Thank you!"

1 cup water
1 stick unsalted butter
1 cup flour
¼ teaspoon salt
Pinch of sugar (optional)
4 eggs

PREHEAT THE OVEN TO 350 DEGREES. In a
medium-size pot, bring the water to a boil and drop
in the stick of butter. Once it's melted, add the flour,
salt, and sugar if you're using it (I usually don't), turn
off the stove, leave the pot on the hot burner, and stir
until the ingredients are combined. They'll form a
nice light-yellow ball of dough.

Add the eggs one at a time, stirring to incorporate
each one completely before adding the next. (Some-
time around the second egg, the average arm will
start to hurt, so it's nice to have someone to turn to
and say, "Will you stir this for me, please?" Thus, the
second monkey.) Once the fourth egg is fully combined, and the batter is one nice ball of dough—none
of which is sticking to the sides or anywhere else—
stir for one more minute. I like an eggy cream puff; if
you like a drier, more classic profiterole, or if you
used extra-jumbo eggs, turn the burner on very low
and stir for another minute to dry out the dough a little. (Should you ever be on a trivia show, this dough
is what the French call a *pâte à choux*.)

With a teaspoon, scoop the dough onto a cookie
sheet, as you would with cookie dough. (If you're

into symmetry, you could use a melon baller or a mini ice-cream scoop, and if you're really feeling fancy you could use a piping bag and push the dough out into thick lines, éclair style.)

Bake for 25 minutes, or until golden brown. The golden brown part is actually very important. If you don't leave the cream puffs in until they form a light crust on top, they'll fall like a soufflé when they hit the kitchen air. (By *crust*, I mean let them make the transition from yellow and delicate to golden with a bit of integrity to them.)

Let them cool on the cookie sheet, then slice them three-quarters of the way through, two-thirds of the way down (so you have a nice cap on a hinge) and fill with your filling of choice. My mother's classic is one box of instant vanilla pudding with only one cup of milk. When it's very thick, add three or four dollops of store-bought whipped cream. Generous dollops get you an airy, light-yellow filling; a lighter touch yields a thicker filling with the denseness of Bavarian cream. Use a teaspoon to fill the cream puffs generously. A dusting of confectioners' sugar at the end, and a few berries on the plate, are a nice addition.

Real whipped cream or ice cream with fresh berries also makes an excellent filling. If you leave out the sugar and fill them with something savory, I've always suspected these could also make very nice appetizers.

T HE TAPAS RESTAURANT DOWN THE STREET SERVES
an *amuse bouche* of pickled garlic, one large, toothpick-
speared bulb for each guest that through some miracle of
vinegar and alchemy is crisp, nearly sweet, and entirely neu-
tralized of any odor. A marvel.

I could make a meal of the sizzling butter that the curled
garlic-shrimp come in, wiping the brown crock clean with soft
bread, and still have room for dessert: a second glass of Albariño
with Manchego and opaque triangles of jewel-colored quince
paste. *Membrillo,* the bartender says, offering its Spanish name.

"I'd be totally happy if I went to a wedding and there were
tapas, cava, wine, and beer," Rich says. "Wouldn't you?"

I would. But then, aren't tapas on a grand scale really just
hors d'oeuvres? Plus, half a dozen plates add up quickly, and
their fee would surely be more than the one-third of our budget that all the magazines recommend spending on the food
portion of a wedding. In keeping with treating this wedding
like a party, there will be no checking of boxes for surf-'n'-turf
or chicken piccata. We want the dinner to be something we'd
really want to sit to. Our first thought was grand-scale takeout

from our favorite Chinatown restaurant (no small gesture, considering my love for its homemade udon, thick as pencils and tossed with shrimp, spinach, and the perfect brown sauce), though surely that would alienate my family. Another thought was a half-Chinese, half-Italian buffet, but in the end that felt more like dividing everyone down the middle instead of bringing them together. Which then brought us back to the original question: What do *we* want to eat?

There's a Spanish community in Newark, New Jersey, just across the Hudson River, and a handful of tapas restaurants; the PATH train, which is as easy as a subway line, goes directly there. Does that make sense? Could someone deliver the food on the morning of the wedding? Could a groomsman pick it up? I stress over logistics for a week until Rich suggests that we try a few places. "If we find something great, we can figure out the details from there," he tells me.

Last night we took the PATH to a somewhat cute, bustling street in Newark's historic Ironbound District, which, judging by the restoration of the train station and the banners on the streetlamps, is begging for a revival. I found a restaurant online with a warm, hearthlike theme, a wall of exposed brick, and a pergola with fake grapes above the entrance to the dining room. We walked there from the train station, passing Latin bakeries and bodegas—and were disappointed to again have our breath hanging in the cold air around us. (What are we thinking, having an outdoor wedding in New Jersey, where the day could as easily dawn fifty degrees as one hundred?)

I wanted so badly to love the food, and to have a good reason to approach the owner, a smiling man with a thick mustache who seemed to have an eye on every forkful entering his guests' mouths. I wanted the problem to be solved, the trip to be a success, the paella to be the best of my life. But none of these was the case.

Tonight we sit to the leftovers: a heavy, tasteless paella, rubbery squid, overcooked shrimp, and a few soggy stuffed mushrooms. We pick at the paella and then wrap it all up with the rest of the cartons and dump it in the trash bin outside, along with our big idea. An hour later, I hear Rich pouring a bowl of cereal, and I join him.

"*Tapas?* What's *tapas?*" my father barks on the phone the following afternoon. I get up and close my office door.

"It's Spanish food. Sausage, potatoes, squid. It's nice—you get to taste lots of different little things."

"*Little things?*" His volume goes up. "Why can't you be like everybody else! You're going to get a tray of ziti, a tray of lasagna, some antipasti, wine, salad. And don't forget whiskey and scotch for the bar," he says. "And anisette for the coffee. You've always got to be different. . . . What's the matter with you?"

Age and his new marriage have mellowed him, but the first mention of the menu and his old temper flashes. It's no secret that few people in my family relate to the idea of graduate school, or to going into so much debt over something so unlikely to produce a living wage. If I'd gone to law school, he once said (joked?), he would have paid. "But this writing business—forget about it." Throw in a Chinese American son-in-law and maybe we have the keys to his irritation.

I take a breath and make myself speak slowly. "We are not having Italian food. If I have a caterer in the boondocks of western New Jersey make ziti and lasagna, it'll taste like we're all eating at Sbarro. You had your wedding"—to keep the peace I resist the plural—"and now it's my turn to have mine. If you want to come and have a nice time, then come. But if you're going to be a bossy jerk, then stay home."

He's muttering swears in Italian, and I can perfectly picture the trio of unhappiness on the other side of the line: the crimson flush, the clenched teeth, and a tight shaking of the head.

"I've got to get back to work," I tell him.

"Well, I'm not eating Chinese food!" is his parting comment.

"Fine."

That night I cut a butternut squash in half, drizzle it with olive oil, put whole garlic cloves in the cavity, and turn it flesh side down on a cookie sheet to roast while I'm at the gym. "Will you please turn off the oven when the timer rings?" I ask Rich on my way out.

He looks up from his laptop, clueless. "What's in there?"

"Butternut squash."

"Aren't you tired of squash? We just ate that."

"Yes, but it's March. The whole country is tired of squash."

"What are you going to do with it?"

"I thought I'd cube it and toss it with white beans and rigatoni."

"*Rigatoni?* I'd rather have penne. Do we have penne?"

"I'm having a hard day," I whine, my temper finally exhausting itself. "I need rigatoni!" Dense and chewy, rigatoni is the most comforting member of the macaroni family.

He laughs a drawn-out "Oh . . ." at my reaction and pushes back his chair to stand and give me a hug. "What happened?"

"My family is insane."

"Is this what I have to look forward to?" I lean my dead weight into him, and he puts little kisses on my forehead.

"Yeah, like that's a surprise. . . . And if you want to back out, just do it now, please, so I can save myself the trouble of renting the stupid tent. Everyone wants to survey the property before quoting a price. I tell them it's a flat acre of empty lawn. How many variables can there be? It's the same tent! Why can't they just quote the price?"

Rich hugs me tighter. "My poor baby," he says, overly ingratiating. "We can eat rigatoni for you."

"Thanks," I tell him flatly. "You're the best."

. . .

I HAVE A SMALL spiral notebook filled with lists, details, and notes, and finally they begin translating into orders. By April we have a tent, tables, chairs, table settings and linens, red and white wines and glass carafes to serve them in, a blow-dry and styling appointment, ten square vases, half a dozen Mason jars, twenty-five dozen orange roses plus three bundles of tiger lilies coming from a South American wholesaler, and enough votive candles to light a bonfire. I narrow down options, Rich and I choose together, and then he writes the checks (at which point our once clever-seeming agreement suddenly feels like the most obvious of scenarios).

The wedding invitations are also in the mail, designed as a wedding gift by Christine, who has just quit her own hated magazine job to start a print and Web-design company. The day's colors will be Popsicle-bright shades of orange, red, and pink, and she worked these into several ideas. In the end, we all agreed on a simple postcard style in bright white and a tidy sans-serif orange font for the text, which is little more than the time, date, and a few lines from the Beach Boys' song "Wouldn't It Be Nice." Centered at the top in red is the Chinese character for double happiness, written and scanned for us by Rich's mother, who as a schoolgirl won awards for her penmanship. But the RSVP cards might be my favorite part: a repeating pattern of the double-happiness character, which, upside down, begins to look like two people holding hands.

The other side of this progress is that Rich is working hard. He's up so late that I sleep for hours, wake to what I think must be morning, and look to find him still working at the kitchen table, with only the dim end-table lamp on. In our open apartment, this has also made him a prime audience to all my sleepwalking and talking. Last night, working at the kitchen table, he noticed me sitting up in bed, glasses on, squinting at the ceiling.

"What's up there?" he asked, suspecting a spider.

"A clear fish, swimming in the dust," I told him, sitting up but still dreaming. I had been reading John McPhee's *The Founding Fish*, about the lives of shad, before falling asleep.

When I walk back to the bed to kiss him goodbye this morning, he reminds me of my antics and the dream floods back in perfect detail. I was conscious enough to see our apartment, and see him, but there was a foot of water hanging from the ceiling and a big, clear fish hiding in some river grass, kicking up a layer of silt. He makes us both laugh, doing an impression of me hastily grabbing for my glasses on the nightstand to more intently stare at the ceiling.

. . .

RICH ISN'T THE only one with a freelance assignment. His sister Alexandra calls me from her office at a daily newspaper and explains they have a "Best Of" issue in the works. "Do you think you can handle Best Cupcake in New York?" she asks. I assure her that I have never been more qualified for an assignment in my life.

I make a list of the city's celebrated cupcake bakers, my favorite bakeries, scan the food message boards, and compile a list of contenders. To reduce variables, I decide my tasting cupcake of choice will be the classic yellow cake with chocolate icing (unless something else looks particularly appealing, in which case, in the interest of fairness, I'll get both). I arrive at work an hour early, leave by five, and head uptown with a plan mapped out. My first stop is Two Little Red Hens on East Eighty-sixth Street, and from there I zigzag back down through midtown (Buttercup, Mitchell London, Blue Smoke), then Chelsea (Amy's Bread, Billy's Bakery), then to Magnolia in the West Village, Sugar Sweet Sunshine in the East Village, and make it home just past eight o'clock, with eight bakery bags holding ten cupcakes.

Rich takes two plates from the cupboard and pours two big glasses of milk. I settle the cupcakes on their wrappers and slice each one into fourths. Then, with my journal beside me, we eat down the line. Neither of us can stop grinning.

"*Mmm . . .*" Rich keeps humming.

The icing on one feels like biting into undisturbed snow. Another is so sweet that I jot down: "My fillings are ringing!" And still another, with a severely smooth layer of dark-chocolate icing, is "Dry, but not dried out—an impressively grown-up cupcake. More than milk, it calls for espresso."

Discrepancies in icing are quickly apparent. One is buttery and smooth, while another is oily, glycerin-slick. We eat and lick fingers and discuss the all-important cake-to-icing ratio. One cupcake is beautifully decorated, but the excess of frosting has to be pushed off onto its waxed paper. Neither of us is a fan of the two very sweetest, and we both fall hard for a chocolate-on-chocolate contender with a chocolate-pudding center—round and heavy as a Magic 8 Ball—but decide it can't be the overall winner, since a criterion of the perfect cupcake should be that a child can hold it.

Of my other favorite of the night, I scribble: "The cake is *white, white* and so moist it nearly feels undercooked. And the smell . . . Is that vanilla? It's like Easy-Bake Oven batter, in the best possible way."

Two nights later, Rich is out at a business dinner and I bring home five more and pour my own milk. While I'm lying on the couch trying to justify to myself that I skipped the gym to eat cupcakes, my mother calls. "Did you have dinner?" she asks. "What did you eat?"

"Half of five cupcakes and two glasses of milk."

"Oh, wow," she says, laughing. This is surprisingly unjudgmental for a woman who, for half my life, only mentioned soda in the same breath as bumper-sticker removal.

"I feel a little sick," I tell her. "But I can't say I didn't enjoy that."

. . .

WE'VE COMBED THE MENUS of the caterers near Bridget's house, but we're nervous about picking one. They all offer too much, too many cuisines—how can they possibly do all of them (any of them?) well? But then one caterer suggests a strawberry-shortcake wedding cake, the lightbulb goes on, and a menu falls into place.

Rich was born in Raleigh, and during my senior year of high school I actually lived there, too. Since we met, I've been hearing that the best strawberry shortcake of his life was in Raleigh at the Capital Room, a cafeteria-style restaurant in the Hudson Belk Department Store. I've been to the particular Hudson Belk he likes to talk about, and in an early essay David Sedaris scrapes trays in a similar Raleigh cafeteria, but Rich's heavy nostalgia for those biscuit-style shortcakes always makes me think, instead, of Calvin Trillin's essay about hometown food nostalgia, and his friend who, "in moments of melancholy or stress or drunkenness, would gain strength merely by staring up at some imaginary storekeeper and saying, in the accent of an Alabama road-gang worker on his five-minute morning break, 'Jes gimme an R.C. and a moon pah.' " For all Rich's day-to-day preferences for clean flavors and light foods, if he can find himself inside a Southern-style restaurant, all is right with the world.

Even the caterer brightens when I mention a Southern menu. This poor woman must be making baked-ziti trays in her sleep, she's so excited by the prospect of chicken and dumplings. Of her own accord, she spends a day experimenting with recipes and then calls us to say they've been a big hit in her storefront business. When she suggests having a chef on site to pan-fry catfish to order, we know she's the one.

We settle on a menu of fried catfish, pulled pork, chicken and dumplings, macaroni and cheese, string beans, collard greens, corn bread, and a strawberry-shortcake wedding cake. When I mail in the deposit, I'm already hungry for it.

"It's funny," Rich says that night. "I don't feel worried about the food at all."

Me neither. Is it because we associate those foods with real kitchens and real people, rather than fancy chefs? Or that I'm excited for the Los Angeles groomsmen to arrive and discover what's for dinner? On special occasions we all used to go to a Southern-style restaurant on Melrose called Georgia; I'm still mourning that it closed its doors several years ago, taking with it the best biscuits of my life. Or maybe, I've just never met a macaroni and cheese I didn't like.

CHAPTER 13

Sickness and Health

PASTINA FOR ONE

BOIL APPROXIMATELY ONE AND A HALF
cups of salted water in a small pot. Add three palmfuls of pastina, lower the flame, and keep the water
at a simmer, stirring occasionally until the water is
absorbed. Add a splash of milk, a pat of butter, a
grating of Parmesan, and salt to taste, and then stir
again until all the liquid is absorbed and the pastina is
soft. Pour the pastina into a shallow soup bowl, put a
thin pat of butter in the center, and drizzle more milk
into one spot until it forms a tiny lake with narrow
rivulets.

Congratulations—you have just made the world's
most comforting food, perfect for a child's lunch or
anyone on the mend. (Note: Some people say milk
isn't good for sick people, but it is impossible to eat
this and not feel better off.)

—

Dinner tonight is blessedly simple, though I feel bad to even say so. We're at the far end of cold season, but Rich calls me at the office to say that he's come down with something, so when I come out of the subway I stop in the Polish diner on our corner. It's a good, clean diner with waitresses who actually smile and all the nice expected bits behind the counter: tall ice-cream-sundae glasses, a milkshake machine, the single-serving cereal boxes that everyone seems to have loved as a kid. A pleated pushpin board, like the kind used in church lobbies for announcements, lists soup specials by the day, as unchanging as my grandmother's regimen. Monday: split pea; white borscht. Tuesday: tomato; lentil. Luckily, chicken noodle, chicken with rice, vegetable, mushroom-barley, and tripe are always on call, each with a country-style slice of buttered challah that's nearly worth the price in itself.

I carry home the warm brown bag, pour the soups into oversized bowls (mushroom-barley for me, chicken noodle for him), and we have a quiet Friday night in front of the television, though Rich has little appetite for either. A few sips are all he manages, and he's in bed by nine. I watch TV in the dark with the volume down low, and then confront, for the first time, the question of whether to sleep in the sickbed or make up the couch and give him room to spread out. Suddenly, sleeping apart from him seems an unbearably lonely prospect. In the end, I opt for the bed and stick to the edge.

You learn a lot about a family by the way they behave when someone is sick. In my family, a sick person is coddled and comforted and made queen for a day. Special meals are prepared for her, and she is allowed to arrange herself and her blankets on the most comfortable stretch of couch, and in a pathetic voice can say things like "Will you lie down with me?" and an otherwise busy adult will stop and offer his or her company. The discomfort of sickness is balanced by an indulgence of attention.

I have two clear memories of being a sick person of elementary-school age. The first is a moment before falling asleep, after being told to take a nap on a day when I wasn't wholly sound but not terribly sick, either. I likely just wanted a day home alone with my mother. The memory is two senses, really. Staring at the pattern of beige and brown amoebas on the couch cushions, and listening to her moving around the kitchen: the clicking of her heels on the floor, the clipped efficiency of her opening and closing cabinets and drawers. Over the years, I've often thought back to the hypnotizing power of those swirling amoebas and the feeling of visualizing the acts that corresponded to her motions, but only recently did it occur to me that the reality of those clicking steps was that she was home with a sick child, in the middle of the afternoon, *wearing heels*. (I will surely be denying my children such glamour.)

The second time, I was genuinely sick and, after a day of keeping nothing down, had woken during the night and called to my mother, who must have had her hands full the day before with the partial installation of a new kitchen floor. The linoleum was torn up to reveal a mess of glue and tacks, and we could step on only a few strategically placed newspaper pages until the men arrived in the morning to lay the floor. She went to the kitchen and I went to the couch, and soon she brought me some Jell-O, which is what people with stomach ailments were given in our house: loosely set Jell-O, or the syrup from canned peaches to sip very slowly. A person with a fever could have pastina with butter and milk, and for colds there was chicken soup with pastina or orzo. My memory is of the newspapers on the floor, the still warm red Jell-O, the Three Stooges on the television at a near-inaudible volume, the niceness of sitting alone on the couch with my mother (who soon fell asleep sitting up), and noticing the day's first light coming up, which was something I had never seen before.

In Rich's house, sick people are given a wide berth. His family stopped going to Christmas mass, he says, because churches are poorly ventilated and therefore prime locations for spreading sickness. "Everyone's always coughing in churches, and they never open the windows," he tells me. "Haven't you noticed that?" A good sick person sequesters herself, washes her hands fervently and often, and touches little. Experiencing Rich's nursing—which, while caring and conscientious, makes a person feel that she has the plague— I've whined, only half joking, "How is a person supposed to get better without any hugs?" The thing about his approach, though, is that it's contagious; once you've been trained to spot sickness in every handshake, it's difficult to undo.

He spends the weekend under a pile of blankets with a fever, and I spend it grazing (a bowl of cereal, a few walnuts and a clementine, some heated-up leftovers), washing the teacups that gradually gather in the sink, and, freed from thinking about or preparing meals, enjoying how much time there suddenly is in the day. By Sunday afternoon, though, his fever's down, but at his insistence he has subsisted on little more than warm broth, and I put my foot down.

"I'm going to make you some pastina."

He takes the thermometer from his mouth and says hopefully, "A little rice gruel would be nice."

He means congee, but he and his sisters enjoy calling it *gruel,* in a drawn-out way that has a ring of Brothers Grimm–style oppression to it. "There's zero nutritional value in rice gruel," I tell him. "You're better off with pastina."

Congee is where my cross-cultural excitement wanes. It is carbohydrates made tangible. You make it by slowly boiling water and cooked rice until every starch molecule has leached out in a goopy ooze. And that's when you eat it. It's like a rice soup, except the soup is its own starch. It's the one food with which a person could stand over the pot and spit into it all day long and in the end it wouldn't look any different.

A business trip once took me to Shanghai, where I ate very nice congee with a dozen little bowls of things to put on top and make it taste like something (or rather, to make it taste exactly like the thing you put on top). But I have little faith in my gruel-making skills. Plus, a bowl of goopy starch seems the last thing a sick person needs in his empty stomach. At least pastina is semolina, a more complex carbohydrate, I reason, and the butter, milk, and Parmesan offer some dairy and protein.

"Please?" he asks.

"No."

I put a little pot of water on to boil, and he calls from behind the couch cushions, flexing the last bit of muscle he still believes himself to possess: "Well, I'm not eating any cheese!"

"Fine," I say.

I make a little extra, pour his portion into a bowl, and add a little cheese to the bit in the pot for me. I set him up on the couch with a napkin, the soup bowl on a big dinner plate, and the television remote. Then I take my bowl back to work at my desk. I hear him take a few bites, and when he says nothing I finally call out, "Well?"

"Oh, very nice," he says conciliatorily.

. . .

WHERE DO OUR IDEAS about what's comforting come from? Is it what we're fed when we're young? When we're sick? Is it the foods of our families? Or is it uniquely coded into us, the stuff of DNA? *What you want when you want it and in the particular combination you fancy.* What makes us fancy what we do?

The right food for me on a Sunday afternoon is pasta in red sauce (always with a scoop of ricotta, if there is some), a romaine salad, and a good yellow semolina bread. Occasionally Rich is up for such a meal, but his palate doesn't itch for it the way mine does, and there's no sadness for him in not waking to the smell of simmering tomatoes.

I love cheese, bread. Could happily eat mozzarella every day, *burrata* at each meal. I suspect that Rich is quietly horrified by how bottomless my appetite for these foods is. His tastes run to cleaner flavors—foods that on the plate look nearly as they did out of the sea or off the tree. "How about baked ziti?" I'll say. "How about sushi?" he'll answer. Though on a miserable winter day he's the first to point us toward the Italian restaurant down the street, the smell of their hand-made pappardelle under rabbit ragù already in his nose.

Maybe the ties of comfort to home are to blame for our

early disconnects over dinner, and for how gracelessly we've merged our households: two peanut butters, two milks, separate shampoos, separate toothpastes. With our own apartments, we could afford to be flexible; after any compromise, stores of our personal necessities waited for each of us at home. Once we shared a home, though, we bristled at the need to still compromise in the one place where the ways in which we adjust to the world are supposed to fall away.

People talk of family as flesh and blood, but once two people throw in their lots together they're family, too. "Isn't it strange that we were two random people in the world, but soon we'll be *family*?" I say to Rich. A family can dream up crazy traditions for, say, celebrating Thanksgiving, or a certain way of eating watermelon, and, should they have a child, he will think that the whole world eats watermelon with a spoon, a quarter melon at a time. That this is not just perfectly natural but the correct way. Forever afterward, if he is offered a flat triangular slice it will make him, even as a grown man, just the slightest bit cranky. Privately, he will wish to be left alone, to be at *home,* to have his fruit served to him the *right* way. We become our family's habits incarnate, and then spend our adult lives reproducing those habits, fighting them, or trying to impose them on the people we newly love.

Maybe the dictator should have made him rice gruel after all.

My mother calls while the day's last light is leaving the room. I'm in the closet working while Rich naps, and I pick up on the first ring. When I mention that Rich is sick, she insists I should make him chicken soup.

"It's Jewish penicillin," she says. I begin to interrupt, loathing this phrase, but she defends herself and keeps going. "I didn't make that up! There's something in the bones . . . I don't know what it is, but it works."

I hate the smell of a boiling chicken carcass—the deep musk that's more decomposition than cooking. Besides, I have a general sense of how chicken soup is made, but not the near-muscle memory of dredging cutlets, sealing calzones— things I've watched her hands do countless times. I learned from my mother mostly what she learned from hers; if I liked what she was making, I'd stand beside her and watch, and always she'd tell me, "Grandma used to say, 'Come see how I do this, so that you can do it when I'm dead.' " Which was very in line with my grandmother's humor.

Once, for a semester, my mother taught an Italian cooking class in the adult-education program at the high school near the Sheppard Place house. She would make dinner for my father, and feed and bathe and get my sisters and me ready for bed, but my father still found it stressful to put the three of us to sleep on his own and after a semester he made her stop. I was too young to remember it, but I know she enjoyed teaching, and somewhere there's a card that her students signed and presented to her with a little booklet of the recipes she'd taught them. Someone brought wine to the last class, and they all had a nice time, laughing and eating what they made, she's told me. In the recipe box I've kept since the night I was allowed to turn on the oven myself, I still have three of the recipes, extra copies, that she distributed to her class. She had typed them out, uppercased and underlined, with a space between each letter:

S T U F F E D   A R T I C H O K E S
Z U C C H I N I   P U F F S
S T U F F E D   E G G P L A N T

I sometimes wonder who they were, those strangers who gathered in the home-economics kitchen around my mother, with her pretty Barbara Eden upsweep. Who can blame them for adoring her, for paying to stand in the kitchen beside her, where she was wonderful? She was unhappy with her decisions, and she tried to make us fear following them, fear becoming her. Though even those strangers could see that she's a perfectly fine thing to aspire to. I'd been listening to her for so long, I'd almost been convinced otherwise.

I decide to head back down the street to the diner. Tonight it's vegetable soup for me and chicken soup with rice for Rich. At the last minute, I think to add a carrot-ginger-apple juice for him, and then take the spinning counter stool closest to the enormous silver juicer by the window. It sends a rush of pleasure over me to walk by here in the mornings when the window is open and catch the bright scent of fresh carrot juice running out of the roaring machine. It's a smell of robustness and good health, though always it reminds me of my brother, whom I never met.

He was diagnosed with leukemia at age three, and passed away when he was seven and my mother was heavily pregnant with me. During those four years, while the doctors bloated him with drugs and radiation, she read books on nutrition and fed him anything she thought might help. "I gave him raw liver," she told me. It lies heavy on her heart. "I puréed raw liver, and he ate it. He'd say, 'Okay, Mommy. Whatever you want me to do.'" A nurse came over twice a day to administer a painful injection. "He'd cry through the whole thing, but he wouldn't budge."

She juiced carrots for him three times a day, sometimes with kale or chard. Later, for us girls, there was occasionally carrot juice on a Saturday, but we were healthy and solid, never a broken bone among us. We liked pushing carrots into the chute of the machine, to provoke the buzz-saw noise of the blade, and to take the first sip of soft foam from the top. His sickness changed the way my sisters and I were raised and fed. Carob instead of chocolate, no white bread, no soda, sugar cereals only as a treat. Food had become a thing that could heal you or harm you, and, if you were lucky, it could maybe even save your life.

I take the juice in one hand and the warm bag of soups in the other. It's an identical parcel from the same waitress as two nights ago, who is kind enough not to mention this. Clearly, there is no cooking going on in my home.

I walk back enjoying the clear night sky, a too-rare thing, and trying to remember the full rhyme for the month of March from the Maurice Sendak book that we read constantly as girls. Bridget's kids have the book now. In it the hero, a dark-haired boy, skates on a winter pond with a crocodile friend, singing monthly tributes to this king of dinners: chicken soup with rice.

STUFFED EGGPLANT

> 2 eggplants (the dark, bulbous type)
> 1/3 cup vegetable oil
> 5 or 6 cloves garlic, minced
> 3 eggs, beaten
> 1/2 cup bread crumbs
> 1/2 to 3/4 cup grated Parmesan cheese (to taste)
> Fresh or dried basil to taste
> Cracked black pepper
> 2 cups marinara sauce

PREHEAT THE OVEN TO 400 DEGREES. Cut the eggplants in half lengthwise and scoop out the insides, keeping the skin intact. Cut the insides into small pieces and soak them in a bowl of salted water for 5 minutes, then drain well. (If I'm in a hurry, I skip the soaking; I've read that the eggplants being grown today aren't nearly as bitter as they used to be.) Heat the oil in a wide pan or pot over a medium flame and add the garlic. Before it colors, add the eggplant, stir, and cook for 10 to 15 minutes, depending on the texture you prefer—you can let the pieces become tender but still somewhat retain their shape, or you can keep cooking until they're almost entirely sludgy and creamy.

Move the pot to a cool burner and add the eggs, bread crumbs, Parmesan, basil, and black pepper.

Cover the bottom of a casserole dish with marinara sauce, set the eggplant skins in the dish, flesh side up, and pour the filling back into them. Top each half with a layer of marinara; if you love a tomato-sensitive person, do this sparingly. Cover with aluminum foil and bake for 35 minutes, then remove the foil and bake for 10 minutes more. Top with grated Parmesan before serving. (For a more delicate version, try replacing the bread crumbs with ricotta.)

CHAPTER 14

Risotto, Frittata, Fried Rice

. . .

WHEN IN NEED OF AN IMPROMPTU MEAL, JAMES BEARD turns to pasta, quiche, and fondues. "Have you ever invited friends to stay for dinner on the spur of the moment and then realized there's practically nothing to eat in the house but eggs and a can of soup?" he wrote in *Beard on Food*. "Of course you have."

Sadly, this is rarely my problem. Nearly everyone I know is incredibly busy, and whatever they do that's impromptu generally only happens after a late round of cocktails. But I do understand the need to occasionally create something from nearly nothing, and at those times I'm learning to turn to risottos, frittatas, and fried rice. In a way, they're three cultures' takes on a theme: a cheap, plentiful something making a few choice bits of something else extend a longer way.

Tonight I've made not a bad fried rice, if I do say so, from the few inches of salmon left from last night's dinner and the leftover bok choy and rice that we ate with it. Rich's mother once noticed that I like the crispy bits of rice from the bottom of the skillet, and she told me approvingly, "It's very Chinese to like that."

When I tell this to Rich now, he asks, "Do you know what that's called?" I shake my head no. "*Gwauh bah.* Literally, it translates to 'pan scab.' "

Such a straightforward language! On our last visit, his mother explained to me that Mandarin doesn't have complicated words like *podiatrist, orthodontist, ophthalmologist.* Instead, the titles translate directly: foot doctor, teeth doctor, eye doctor. "So many extra *words* in English!" she'd said, and hung her head in the cute way she does—an *aw shucks* gesture I imagine she picked up from films.

Tonight's fried rice also receives high praise from Rich, who now leans back from it. While I remain intent on my plate, he has a habit of taking a little digestive respite midway through a meal—long enough that I nearly always begin to wonder if he's finished—before leaning back in to begin again. Sitting back now, he asks, "Do white people know that fried rice is made with leftover rice?"

"I don't know," I answer on behalf of all white people. "It's not really something you think about until you try to make it."

"White people order fried rice as an entrée," he continues, explanatorily. "It's only *on* the menu for them. Chinese people order white rice *with* their entrée—a real entrée—and then take home the leftovers and make fried rice."

I hadn't thought much about it before my first attempt at fried rice, from a recipe in the *LA Times.* All those years ago I must have left a page in the office printer, because the first page, now splattered with stains, is an ingredients list and the first three steps, and the next page is a single line of plating instructions. I'd still be interested to know what that second page said, but fried rice is a forgiving dish and I've learned to make do without it. My mainstays are garlic, eggs, salt, pepper, and drizzles of soy sauce, sesame oil, oyster sauce, and Sriracha. I start with two tablespoons of hot oil in the skillet, add garlic and two eggs and scramble them until they're nearly cooked. Then I remove the eggs, add more oil and garlic, and sauté whatever vegetables I'm using—asparagus, peas, string beans, carrots, zucchini. Just about anything works, on its own or together. When the vegetables are nearly finished, I add the chopped protein (usually a bit of leftover fish) plus the leftover rice to warm up, and then return the eggs to the skillet. When it's all hot, I drizzle the sauces over it, add salt and pepper to taste, stir again, and let it cook for one more minute so that the bottom can crisp up. From Rich I learned to use some salt instead of relying entirely on soy sauce for the sodium, which he says makes it "too soy-saucey."

If there are scallions in the crisper, still dry and maintaining their integrity, I chop and sprinkle them over the top at the end. If there isn't leftover fish in the house, I'll add an extra egg and let that be the sole protein; or if we have tofu I'll dry it, cube it, and then fry it in a few tablespoons of oil to put a golden crust on the sides. Then I let it rest on a paper towel, use the tofu oil to scramble the eggs in, go about business as usual, and add the tofu at the end before the sauces. (The best part of this is the dance the tofu does, even once it's set on the paper towel, a series of twitches and jerks that seem to originate in their small centers.)

Rich's point about the old rice is a good one; fresh rice

is too moist and won't separate and fry up properly, the same way that bread pudding does best with stale bread. They're dishes born of ingenuity—devised for using what's on hand—that trick that both the Chinese and the Italians are good at. Though Rich's father has his own ideas about what our cultures have in common. "Americans serve the worst possible versions of both our cuisines," he told Rich once. "But when you find the real things, there's nothing better."

Fried rice also fits in the wonderful, quirky genre of foods that only come from a leftover dish—not just an ingredient, like stale bread, but a finished dish that begets another. *Arancini* only come from leftover risotto. And my mother's potato croquettes, a similar concept to *arancini*, make excellent appetizers the night after mashed potatoes. Just add eggs, Parmesan, seasoning, and maybe some chopped prosciutto to the cold, lumpy potatoes, roll spoonfuls into a shape like a thick index finger, dredge them in bread crumbs, and fry them in hot oil until golden brown.

I'm also learning to pull a risotto together from whatever is in the house, as long as I remember to keep vegetable stock in the pantry. (A friend returned from Italy with a gift of mushroom bouillon cubes, somehow so much better than their American counterparts, that make an outrageously good stock. We've been using them as reverentially as saffron.) Swiss chard, a few plump shrimp, artichoke hearts, even the never-say-die kale that unfailingly appears in the winter stalls of the farmers' market makes for a good risotto. Rich sometimes also makes a version using the sardine-style tins of *pulpo*, baby squid, that we find in the Mexican bodega.

With a kick of heat from Sriracha or chilies, it's a good last-minute dinner.

We once spent a week in Tuscany, in a teeny hotel where the dinner was included, and it took us three nights of falling asleep in our clothes within minutes of climbing the stairs to our room to realize that the heavenly risotto was to blame. A good stock relieves the need for much, or any, butter; though in *Molto Italiano,* Mario Batali writes that to keep things light he'll sometimes even use water instead of stock. Butter or mascarpone is nice on a special occasion, but on nights when we'd like to stay conscious for a few more hours, a drizzle of olive oil and a handful of grated Parmesan at the end work to good results.

Frittatas, too, require only eggs and imagination. Any cheese, any vegetable, any fresh herb, or even other proteins (salmon, ham, pepperoni) will work; it's hard to make a poor match. My favorites are zucchini with basil, or potatoes with green peppers cooked to nearly melting. I just sauté the vegetables, add them to a bowl of beaten eggs with herbs, salt, pepper, and sometimes cheese, and pour it into a hot skillet over a medium flame. When the eggs are mostly cooked, I put a plate over the skillet, flip the two in one controlled motion, and then slide the frittata back into the skillet, loose side down. With a tossed salad and good bread, it's one of my favorite dinners—though Rich finds it light and prefers it as a Saturday lunch.

Our friend Alessandra once brought a frittata to a Fourth of July picnic. Eggs are the last thing I would have thought to bring, but of course she knew better. We were under trees, with the sun going down, and it made our cobbled contributions—fruit, cheese, cured meats, bread, wine—suddenly seem a complete meal. Plus, it's good warm or cold.

While these three flexible entrées have helped keep us fed lately, with Rich there's never a foolproof plan. I'm just back from the gym, stretching in my sweaty clothes outside the bathroom door, when he looks up from his computer and asks, "What should we do about dinner?" He says it in a tone that means he's wishing he could pop a Jetsons-style pill and be done with it: all the taste and calories of a steak dinner in one efficient swallow.

He has an assignment due tomorrow that he's still researching. The writing itself, and his own drive to dot every *i*, are taxing in themselves, but lately the presence of online comment sections heightens the inherent stress. Instant feedback! Anyone with an opinion and an email address can berate you before a forum of millions, whether you're stating opinions or triple-checked facts. More than ever, comments seem hit-first-think-later combative, self-righteous, rude. I can't help feeling that they're a gauge of the city's temperament, and we're at a high boil. Normally, this is a topic for dinner-table discussion, but tonight it's just cause for stress.

"How about an udon noodle soup with mushrooms and baby bok choy?" It's Tuesday, and I went to Pitts on Friday evening, but only to quickly pick up eggs, milk, and bread for the morning. I meant to order groceries online on Sunday night, but I never got around to it.

He scrunches up his face. "That sounds filling for about five minutes."

"I could slice a boiled egg on top."

"I need more food than that," he says. Then, after a pause, "What kind of mushrooms do we have?"

"I don't know, shiitake? You bought them."

"The ones I bought last week? Are those still good?"

"I think so. I don't know, I didn't look that closely. How about a butternut-squash soup, and then gemelli with mushrooms?"

"That sounds like a lot of work, for still not a whole lot of food."

"And I guess no protein, really . . . *Or* we could toss the squash with pasta, and I think there's enough spinach for a salad with mushrooms and a boiled egg." I'm actually enjoying this; three months ago I would have stopped at the udon.

"I'm kind of pasta'd out," he says.

"How about a spinach-mushroom frittata with roasted fingerling potatoes?" *Roasted* and *potatoes* tend to be winning words in a conversation like this.

"Are those potatoes still good?"

"I think so. *Or* I could make onion soup, although I've never really done that before . . . with cheese, and a little bruschetta and a salad. I bought a really nice half-goat, half-sheep cheese.

"But then we're back to soup, which isn't really filling. Why are you so stuck on soup?"

"Well, there's a carton of stock already open. It only lasts seven days."

"Actually, I could really stand to get out of the house," he says, pushing back his stool to stand up and stretch. "Do you want to just go out?"

My mind is still working through the onion-soup idea. Do

we have the kind of bowls that can go into the oven? Though I guess even if we did, the cooked-on cheese would be a nightmare to wash off. "Sure," I say, turning on the shower. "Where do you want to go?" And we play our game of back-and-forth again.

. . .

APRIL IS ALWAYS a busy month. On my current to-do list are gifts for Bridget, my friend Erin, my mother, and my stepmother, all of whom have birthdays within a span of four days. I also need to find wedding bands, write up directions for guests who are leaving the city by train, figure out the seating chart, and print out table numbers, which, after a bit of fiddling with the design, will be another gesture toward merging everyone—the Chinese double-happiness character above the table number spelled out in Italian. If nothing else, it'll appease my father, who was upset that the invitations seemed more *them* than *us*. (That I've decided to keep my name has gone without comment, but a Chinese icon on some stationery warranted a special call.)

My journal has entire weeks missing from it, and I've started trading my morning writing for morning workouts, which for some reason make more of an impact. I've been watching my dinner portions, skipping the half-and-half in my coffee, resisting the free roll with my lunch salads, and finally I'm down four pounds. (Who am I to buck this American rite of passage, I joked to Rich recently, trying to make light of the subject of weight. Dieting, to my mind, is a thing to be done among women and kept from the thoughts of men.) At the bottom of the list is a reminder to send out two rejected essays to new journals. One editor replied that he liked the writing but not the topic, and the other, at the journal I love most, sent a rejection letter full of compliments, which still stung.

"I can't *wait* until this wedding is over," Rich says with a sigh, falling into bed, and I know exactly what he means.

Tonight I leave work late, wanting to finish an article so the editor in chief, who arrives early, can begin editing it first thing. "Go home!" Kay says, poking her smiling face, wrapped in hat and scarf, in my office doorway.

"I'm going, I'm going!" I call after her. A moment later I hear her key turn the deadbolt—a sound that always returns me to the Sheppard Place house and hearing my father, leaving for work in the dark, turning on the front porch to lock the final lock behind him. It's a sound of being protected, loved.

Emerging from the subway later, I stop at the Polish bakery, where the nighttime batch of bread has just come from the oven. I buy a loaf of unimaginably soft buttermilk-wheat, still too hot to slice. At home I putter around, trying to shake off the day, and throw in some laundry. We each do our own, which is the single satisfying way in which all the domestic chores have not fallen to me. Some days, I'll find a few of my things on the bed that Rich washed with his and then folded into inexplicably tiny packages. Finally ready to confront dinner, I offer him a few options, none very inspired.

"Actually," he says with a boyish smile, "I would kind of like a sandwich. I can't stop thinking about that bread." I opened the bag to let the steam out when I got home, and its scent has lightly filled the kitchen.

I bought hummus this week, which I slather onto my slices, cut thick and country style, with tomato, lettuce, slippery roasted red peppers, and an oval of creamy-white provolone. He has the same, minus the hummus and plus a few slices of salami and ham with a slick of mayonnaise. The crackle of the lettuce, as he halves each of our sandwiches with the big serrated bread knife, is a perfect sound. Two dill-pickle spears apiece and we sit down almost giddy.

On the rare night that the stars are aligned, it seems there can be a dinner even simpler than risotto, frittata, or fried rice.

...

WORK SENDS ME ON A LONG TRAIN RIDE INTO NEW Jersey on a day that starts out sunny but devolves into freezing rain. When I finally emerge from the Bedford station—twelve hours, one round-trip New Jersey Transit ride, and four subway connections later—the rain is lashing and the cold bites through my light-blue spring raincoat, a gift from Maria. There's a blister on my left heel; I'm exhausted, hungry, and naggingly aware that Rich invited his sister Alexandra to dinner. She lives downtown, beside the Seaport, which as the crow flies is a mile away; the subway ride takes forty minutes, though, and, with the long hours she works, we rarely see her.

I call Rich from under an awning. "Well, is she coming?" I ask, the wind whipping over the mouthpiece. "And what are we going to feed her?"

"I'm not sure, I haven't heard from her," he says. Then, "What's that noise? Where are you?" He's snug inside our living room, oblivious to the elements. Angling my umbrella, I make my way down Bedford toward the Depressed Grocer and, blowing in with the wind, drop my dripping umbrella on the cardboard mat beside the door.

"It's awful out there!" I complain, almost before I'm aware of the words leaving me.

"In here, it is not so bad," she says, smiling slightly. Is she wearing makeup? The boom box on a high shelf with the toilet paper is playing a good hip-shaking song by a Lebanese band I recognize from one of Yasmine's dance mixes, and after a moment I become aware of a man somewhere back in the storage room, whistling along. Well, good for her, I think. Then I buy a box of thick spaghetti, two cans of clams, and trudge home through the rain, which is managing to blow from all sides.

At our building, an impressive stream courses off the short metal awning, and it takes some maneuvering to work the key into the lock while keeping my laptop bag and purse from taking a dip. I stamp my way to the middle security door, trying to rid myself of some water, and drop the umbrella with a clatter outside our apartment. The door swings open and Rich greets me with an overly big smile—a puppy who's been left home alone all day. He takes my purse, laptop bag, dripping raincoat, and wet groceries while I kick off my shoes into the small pile by the door. I stand there for a moment, making the exaggerated pouting face I learned from him, so cranky I could burst.

Quickly putting down my things, he returns to give me a long hug. Part of my brain registers that it's nice that when I'm having a meltdown his mood can correspondingly slide in the opposite direction, evening us out. Finally, his lips in my hair, he says, "I think a nap may be in order." I lie down on the couch and he puts the silk throw pillow that Maria once sewed for me under my head and covers me with the blanket that I cover him with when he's napping. Then he turns off the overhead light, clicks on the soft lamp, and I'm nearly asleep before he tiptoes away.

Forty-five minutes later, I wake to the smells of garlic and cream and a toasty warm apartment. I sit up a little to see what he's doing, and, noticing me, he says, "How's my baby feeling? Better?"

The table is nicely set for three, with candles and delicate-stemmed wineglasses—a wedding gift that's arrived in the mail—and he's working happily at the cutting board while managing two burners at the stove. I don't know if there's a salad, and I don't care; I'm learning to enjoy the sensation of fully handing over the controls. *This is a good man,* I tell myself.

"Yes," I say, lying back down. "Much better, thanks." Then, remembering, I sit back up. "I think the Depressed Grocer has a boyfriend!"

"Oh, excellent!" He smiles. "Good for her."

. . .

THIS HAS BEEN an April of extremes. Two days ago a burst of heat returned, hovering in the eighties and making us drag (too literally) the air conditioner from the coat closet. For tomorrow, the prediction is low fifties. But leaving the office today it's a breezy seventy-two, with everyone on the sidewalks after work united by the elated look of spring fever on our faces. Such bliss to have the sun still high at 6 P.M.! The trees along Lexington Avenue have overnight come alive with white petals that snow down with each breeze.

I used to dream of an autumn wedding—my favorite season by far—but a spring wedding has begun to seem just right. The entire city feels ready to turn the page and begin a new chapter, and as clichéd as it sounds when the words come to me—*turning the page*—I'm feeling ready to as well.

We have a restaurant and a menu confirmed for the rehearsal dinner, which will be casual and cocktail-party style, so everyone arriving from out of town can mingle and catch up. Rich also has new wedding clothes that he's happy about: his first high-end dress shirt from a good London shirtmaker and a navy slim-fitting Italian suit that somehow makes his cheekbones look even sharper. *Dashing* is the first and only word that comes to mind. I've reserved a block of rooms at a hotel near Bridget, which isn't nearly as hokey as I'd feared. A photographer friend of our upstairs neighbor is going to take photos, and I finally have the last of the gifts for the wedding party. The only thing left on the list is a wedding band for me.

We picked out a band for Rich last night, eating bowls of ramen noodles side by side in front of his computer, before running out to a friend's art opening. He showed me a few sites he'd found, and we both liked one particular stainless-steel band. It's simple but handsome. He's not a ring wearer, but he seems pleased about the idea of wearing this one. I think it suits him better than the chunky gold bands I've begun noticing on the ring fingers of my male colleagues, and I like that its brushed exterior will gradually nick and weather and take on a new look; that time will change it but make it more beautiful seems in keeping with the sentiment of marriage.

I was hoping to buy my band from the shop in Los Angeles where Rich picked out my engagement ring with Maria, but there hasn't been time for a trip. I don't mind buying one after the wedding, on our next visit out (surely someone will assure me this is bad luck), but I still need something to get married with.

Between the office and the subway is an ugly little jewelry store, and tonight when I go past I ring the bell and am buzzed in. Display cases run along one long wall, and in the back three women are standing around a counter, chewing hard on their gum. "Do you have a cheap, plain, silver-looking ring?" I ask. They look at one another, and then one pulls away from the group and walks lethargically to the case closest to the door. She runs a heavily decorated fingernail over a selection of rings pushed into velvety gray holders, and then holds up a shiny, silver-colored band. "This one's $6.99," she says.

Final item, check. I hand over seven dollars, she puts the ring in a gray velvet ring box, and I say a silent prayer that no unsuspecting woman ever opens a box like this to a ring like that.

Beside the entrance to the Fifty-third Street subway station, a produce cart has a pile of frying peppers in high shine. They're the green of a newly unfurled leaf, nearly bright as highlighter pens. I like these peppers stuffed with the same bread crumb mixture my mother drizzles into artichokes—a cup of bread crumbs, a cup of grated cheese, two eggs, half a cup of water, a stream of vegetable oil, and basil or parsley—and then slow-cooked in a skillet. Their skins brown and soften, pull away from the bright-green flesh, and slide off with a little tug. Plus, some magic happens overnight that makes them even sweeter the next day, eaten cold for lunch.

There's half a focaccia on the counter from the farmers' market on Saturday, and mesclun and frisée in the salad spinner. I can make a salad with the honey goat cheese I bought yesterday and the last of the dried figs from the dinner party.

Halfway down the subway stairs my phone rings, and I run back up to catch the call.

"Hi, babe!" my mother says. "I finally found something to wear!" For Bridget's wedding she didn't find a dress until the final hour, a beautiful one-shouldered white gown with a spray of copper and gold sequins. My sister had complained, "Only the *bride* should wear white!" But she could show up in the same dress I'm wearing, for all I care; these days my stresses are focused on Wes's having a working toilet installed, the sun staying out, and my father not terrifying Rich's sweet, quiet family with his booming voice and unpredictable antics.

"It's a suit," she says, "in a kind of light green. I didn't see anything in the store, but then walking back to the car I spotted it in the window." She pauses. "I think it might actually look nice."

"That sounds perfect!" I tell her. "I can't wait to see it!" I can hear that she's smiling, and I'm glad. I feel bad that she'll be dateless at the wedding, while my father has his new wife. Who, actually, is very nice.

A taxi driver is laying on his horn, facing off with a crosstown bus trying to maneuver around a temporary steam pipe. "Well, I'll let you go," she says. "I can hear that you're busy." But I'm not quite ready to let her go.

"Everything else is mostly ready," I say, raising my voice above the noise. "I think it's going to be okay."

"I'm sure it's going to be beautiful," she says. "I'm really looking forward to it."

Hanging up, I catch myself smiling. Maybe that's the final check on my list. In every regard I have always been my mother's daughter, choosing what she ushered me toward. But in order to find *me*—"the authentic self," as Heidegger called it, the self we work to become, versus the person our environments will more easily shape us into—I had to take a step away from her. Which was hard on both of us. Slowly, though, we're finding a way back toward each other.

. . .

THE FIRST MONDAY in May, and I wake with a plan. When the alarm clicks on at six-thirty, I take the phone into the bathroom, trying not to wake Rich, and leave a voice mail for my editor saying that I'm taking a sick day. With the pages flying off the calendar, there has been no time to write, and I need a day to dig out my old self and regroup. (We're postponing the honeymoon until August, so I'll be out of the office for only a few days. I suspect he won't mind.)

For maximum efficiency, I decide to treat the day like a workday: a run, into the shower, and then at my desk by nine o'clock. Trying to help me with my terrible tennis backhand, Rich will sometimes tell me to visualize myself swinging: to embed, behind my eyelids, a little video of myself performing perfectly, so that reality has something to follow. Brushing my teeth now, I visualize myself working steadfastly through the day, piling up good, solid pages on my desk while delivery boys on bicycles come and go with meals I simply have no time to prepare. I quietly lock the front door behind me and head out running south.

A certain type of New Yorker likes to insist on never traveling above Fourteenth Street, but my Columbia apartment was on 119th—a no-man's-land by cool-kid standards, but close to both Central Park and Riverside Park, which were perfect for running. Riverside is all about the water, with its cherry-blossom path following the line of the Hudson and rows of rocking boats docked in the Boat Basin, which is soothing on the eyes in every light and weather. In Central Park, however, the emphasis is on the earth: the soil scent of the bridle paths; the piles of golden gingko leaves come October; and the lush, humid *greenness* of its summertime canopy, the old trees stretching to form a cool funnel over even its widest roads. The parks were my respite when I felt my tolerance for concrete waning.

In Williamsburg, my route is up and over the bridge, around the first Lower East Side street sign, and back over. It doesn't have the same refreshing effect, but the view from the bridge lifts the heart in its own way. I head up the incline on the south-side pedestrian pathway, away from the yellow husk of the shuttered Domino Sugar factory. To my left, farther south on the water, is the steel blue of the Manhattan Bridge and, beyond it, as the tip of Manhattan curves west, the Brooklyn Bridge, with its brick archways and photogenic good looks. By comparison, the Williamsburg is their working-class cousin, smocked in institutional gray. The J, M, Z subway line barrels down its center, cars swish by on either side (westbound to the north, east to the south), and above the traffic lanes the pedestrian walkways are painted red steel, with large faded swaths of Pepto-Bismol pink.

My father, imagining the Williamsburg of thirty, or maybe ten, years ago, barks, "You run across that bridge? Are you crazy!" But in the evenings, especially, the walkways are filled with bicyclists, joggers, and rollerbladers. The neighborhood south of the bridge is largely home to Hasidic Jews, and I pass entire families out strolling with baby carriages and small children, the group traveling the pace of the smallest child. The women wear churchy blouses with modest navy or black skirts, hats or wigs or both, and have a peacefulness about them that's striking; though their husbands, with their soft stomachs and shapeless black suits in every weather, look to me interchangeable.

The men occupy a world of their own, but it surprises me, too, the way even the women, guiding their children out of the running path, avoid my eyes. In my yoga pants and a tank top, I wonder if I offend them. I still think back with embarrassment to the audacity with which I ran through Regent's Park, during a semester abroad in London, in just a sports bra and shorts (twenty-one years old and all confidence, with a washboard stomach I'd crunched my way to that summer), past women in full hijabs. I'd felt free and empowered and pitied them how trapped they seemed. Now I shudder at my younger self and what they must have thought of me.

Reaching the traffic island on the Manhattan side, I make a narrow turn around a street sign, its backside studded with chewing gum, and head back up and over, trying to maintain my pace. A guy coming toward me on a bicycle, scruffy beard, handsome, and about my age, smiles as he goes past. There's one old boyfriend whom I think of sometimes and half expect to bump into. I adored him, and he had a close, sweet family any girl would be lucky to inherit; but I was nineteen, twenty, far from wanting to be married and somehow still terrified I would marry him and wind up living out my days in the same square mile where I'd grown up. When all I wanted was to get out.

Who would I be now if I'd stayed with him? He was the only son in a family of three daughters—the prince—which worried me. Though who could be more of a prince than the only son in a Chinese family?

She was so in love, she simply couldn't see.

Who will I become in this marriage? And why does it always feel to me a leap, a test. That I'll say "I do" and the answer, like a magic trick, will be revealed: wrong or right. The veil was lifted and my mother says she saw the answer clearly, but I've stopped believing in this. I want whatever happens to be the outcome of the two of us and our years together, not a thing predetermined by a single choice: a melon to split open and see how I fared. All my life I've wrangled for control, not trusting others to do a job right. How many group projects did I take home in school, offering to do the extra work myself, for the assurance of the outcome I was after? But with this I have to let go and trust Rich with his half. For the first time, seeing to every detail myself will create the opposite of the result I'm after.

On the steep descent back to Brooklyn, I let gravity pull me faster, still hearing the instructions of the high school cross-country coach, his clipboard cinched at his side: "Be like a rolling rubber tire."

Rilke deserves better company, but in my stream-of-consciousness running brain, it's he who comes to me next. "Be patient toward all that is unsolved in your heart," he advised a conflicted young poet, "and try to love the questions themselves like locked rooms and like books that are written in a very foreign tongue."

At three-thirty, I sit down at my desk with a second cup of coffee and listen to Rich finish up a call with our friend

Matsu, who has just returned from his first solo show in Japan. When he hangs up I call out, "How did it go?"

Rich walks back to my desk smiling and nodding, in a little stooped-over way that he first began doing as an impression of his father, though now I wonder whether he even realizes he's doing it. "It sounds like it went really well—he said he sold a lot of pieces. I'm really happy for him. . . ." he says. "We should get together for dinner soon."

And that's really all it takes. The merest whiff of a dinner party and my undisciplined thoughts run off to table settings, first courses, dessert. Broccoli rabe was on sale this week, so I bought two bunches, and there's a big eggplant in the crisper that I've been wanting to stuff, which is the only preparation of eggplant we've found that doesn't make Rich's tongue itch. We've even managed to keep a few unopened bottles of wine in the house.

"Well . . . do you want to ask him to dinner?" Matsu has been saying that he'll make us a Japanese meal if I make him an Italian one. "It doesn't get more Italian than broccoli rabe, and I could stuff that eggplant and cut it into quarters as a first course."

I'm expecting Rich to be the voice of reason, his usual role when I careen us toward spontaneous plans, but instead he says, as if it were the first half of an equation, "We can't really invite him and not give him any meat."

"I could get some more prosciutto, and you guys could have it with arugula and Parmigiano-Reggiano. That would make a nice salad."

"How about an antipasti platter?" he counters, which would be easy enough. We already have aged provolone, roasted peppers, and marinated artichokes. Rich calls Matsu back and he accepts, then we think to invite the upstairs neighbor, and suddenly we are four for dinner at seven o'clock.

A few days ago Rich said to me, teasingly, "For someone so interested in not perpetuating gender roles, you manage to put yourself in the kitchen at every chance." I protested, but as soon as he said it I knew he was right. Despite my insistence that I don't want to be the family cook, I can no more stay out of the kitchen than I can look at an unmade bed; it's hardwired into me.

Later, after his comment, something clicked. Was taking on the cooking as my contribution to the wedding effort a ruse? Had I given myself an excuse to be the person in the kitchen, doing the thing I swore that in a marriage I never would? I'm a little stunned that I could dupe myself so easily. Or that I'd need to. Duped or not, though, it's been good for us. I'm learning to do things—drop clothes at the dry cleaner, stop in the bakery, run an errand at the hardware store—without keeping score, or wondering if I'm the one doing more. (When I'm ugly enough to bring this up, it usually turns out that I'm not; Rich is just nicer about doing little jobs without broadcasting that they've been done.) Which is the definition of faith, really: "the assurance of things hoped for, the conviction of things not seen," as Hebrews 11:1 puts it.

I sometimes wonder what would have happened if someone had whispered to me that January day in Los Angeles, as I busied myself and Rich waited for his interview, that this was the man I was going to marry. It's the kind of self-sabotaging information people are privy to in movies and that changes all their steps going forward, sending them down a new path. All the thinking I've been doing these last seven years, all the wondering. What if someone could simply have told me: *This is the one.*

I suppose I wouldn't have believed it.

To sit by seven, I'll need a half hour to run to Pitts and back, and if I can't make dinner in an hour, then I'm truly a fool for doing this. That means I can work until five-thirty, which I make myself sit and do. Then I head to Pitts and buy prosciutto, bresaola, olives, and ciabatta to round out the antipasti platter. Standing in the market, I consider making cream puffs for dessert but then force myself to keep things simpler still and buy strawberries and good vanilla ice cream instead—a very Yasmine dessert. From her I've learned to serve it in the most beautiful bowls possible, paying proper due to this most classic of combinations: strawberries and cream.

At home, I wash and trim the broccoli rabe and then score and scoop out the eggplant halves. Then I soak their innards in salted water and leave them to drain. Rich sets the table, arranges the antipasti on a big white platter, and then slices and sugars the strawberries so they break down and grow sweeter before it's time to serve them. I chop enough garlic for both dishes, sauté the eggplant in olive oil and garlic until it's soft, then take it off the flame and add bread crumbs, grated cheese, two eggs, and dried parsley. Then the mixture goes back into the hollowed skins and is topped with a bit of sauce. Rich straightens up the living room, putting stray socks in the hamper and water glasses in the sink. I slice a lemon and fill a carafe with water for the table, put the eggplant in the oven, sauté the broccoli rabe in garlic, and set it aside. He washes the dishes I've used so far and then opens the wine, and I set a pot of salted water on the back burner, which I'll start up once our guests arrive, and we're finished. The kitchen is tidied, the set table looks pretty with the colorful antipasti at its center, and, miraculously, there's time for a glass of wine before they arrive.

We sit back into the couch and prop our feet side by side on the coffee table. "Not a bad team," I say.

"Not bad at all," he says, swirling his wine. Then he lifts his glass to me. "To the chef, *salud*."

"*Salud*," I repeat, raising my glass. "*Cent'anni*." I like this toast, to "a hundred years." It's probably more appropriate for birthdays or anniversaries, but I like the idea of toasting to that much happiness.

"A hundred years, huh?" Rich says, absorbing the words. "You think we can make it that long?" After all the marriage fears I've expressed, this is the first tip of his hat toward having similar anxieties.

What if someone could whisper in our ears right now? Could tell us that in five years, or fifty years, we'll be as happy as we are now—or to get out quick and run. What would we do if we could know what happens from here?

I touch my glass to his, and it rings out a clear, bright note.

Acknowledgments

...

Acknowledge feels too weak a word for the down-on-my-knees groveling thanks I owe to so many people for their help, encouragement, guidance, and love.

I can't say thank you enough to Lea Beresford, at Random House, whose efforts and enthusiasm exceeded my every hope. Thank you so much for believing in this book—it's a kindness I will always be grateful for.

Byrd Leavell at the Waxman Agency, in addition to being a man whose cool I aspire to, is an agent extraordinaire: thank you for seeing I had this book in me, and for coaxing it out.

Thank you to Colette Vella at Murdoch for the introduction to Australia, and to Jane von Mehren at Random House for the push when I needed pushing.

Thank you to Alex French, Christine Castro, Mina Cheong, Helen Coster, and Kamy Wicoff for their friendship and excellent edits, and to Tina French and Lisbet Gutierrez for their cheerleading. To Michael Anderson, who has guided my writing and my wine education in ways I'm unworthy of but enormously grateful for: say the word, and there's *Epoisses* with your name on it.

Enormous hugs to Erin, Alex, Alexandra, Christine, Tee Tee, and the real-life Catherine, Yasmine, Patrik, James, Allison, Paolo, and Alessandra for being wonderful muses. (And if you didn't know you were in here, I really hope you didn't mind when you found out.)

To my new extended family, whom I'm so grateful that Rich came complete with: *Xie xie* for your boundless support!

My love and thanks to Wes, whom I can only hope to someday repay for the hospitality and the vodka; to Bridget, for all her hard work, as well as the imparting of several essential life skills; and to Maria for her early edits, faithful visits, and excellent eye: there's no one I'd rather share a brain with.

To my parents, who haven't read a word of this book as I sit writing this page: I hope you'll read this as the love letter that it is. At its center, this story is a celebration of the beautiful childhood you gave me, and of the love you poured into me, and the unmatchable richness, craziness, and texture of our family—without which I wouldn't have the confidence or wherewithal to so intentionally inspect each experience and determine who it is I want to be.

And lastly, of course, I'd like to thank Rich, without whom none of this would be possible—for his patience, friendship, support, and love—though words feel suddenly inadequate. To you, I give my whole heart.

MICHELLE MAISTO has an MFA in nonfiction writing from Columbia University, and her work has appeared or is forthcoming in a number of publications, including *The New York Times* and *Gourmet* magazine. She writes and eats in Brooklyn, New York, with her husband, Rich, who occasionally does the cooking.